Teatro Izcalli Presents

Nopal Boy
&
Other Actos

By Macedonio Arteaga Jr. & Teatro Izcalli

ISBN 1-934379-94-8

Teatro Izcalli

CONTENTS

Teatro Izcalli

In Loving Memory Of

Maria Anguiano
and
Victor "El Ruq" Chavez

SIN VERGUENZA,
A FORM OF GRATITUDE

When we first started the group, Alicia Chavez and I went out to dinner and we began to write some sketches on napkins. We had no idea exactly how to write comedy sketches, but we did the best we could. For a couple of them we used mainstream movies and tv shows and twisted them to create our own Chicano version. This all happened after we were inspired by a Chicano comedy troupe known as Culture Clash. That was the beginning of our journey. So a very special thank you has to be extended to all of the past Teatro Izcalli members who I've had the honor to share the stage with; Luis Gomez, Abel Macias, Benny Madera, Alejandro Ochoa, Maria Santos, Miguel-Angel Soria, Victor Chavez Jr., Maria Figueroa, Ricky Medina, Cristina Nuñez, and Michelle Tellez. Also thank you all of you who worked on certain projects with us; Aldo Aleman, Sylvia Romo-Lara, Jesse Payan, Ramon "Chunky" Sanchez, Olympia Rodriguez, Gabriel Nuñez, Ohtli Romo-Lara, Layla Baily, and Veronica Burgess.

Many people have been a part of Teatro Izcalli's journey, far too many to mention on this short page. So I apologize beforehand for not listing everyone's name. I will simply have to say thank you to all of you who have helped us over the years with various duties, Sandra Soria, Jose Alvarado, Victor Ochoa, Armando Nuñez, Albert Rascon, Carlos Solorio, Marta Flores, Jessie Perez, Veronica Aranda, Ashley Lucas to name a few. All of you who worked on set designs, props, make-up, stage hands, understudies, sound, music, video, photography, graphic art, translations, editing, and so much more. We couldn't have done it without you. Thank you to Izcalli, the Centro Cultural de la Raza, the community, and most importantly to our families and friends who have supported our work for the past 13 years. Last and not least a very important thank you has to be extended to Profe Jorge Huerta for all of his help and encouragement over the years.

We're now at this important milestone because of the hard work and dedication of our current group members many of whom have been with the group since the beginning; Iyari Arteaga,

1

Alicia Chavez, Claudia Cuevas, Jose Alvarez, Mike Slomanson, and Hector Villegas. Our goal has always been to inspire students to continue to carry the voice of the oppressed and the voice of Chicano Theater. As you will find some of these actos are very political and some were created just for laughs. As Luis Valdez and Culture Clash influenced us, we hope our work influences the next generation as well. ¡Que viva el Teatro!

~ Macedonio Arteaga Jr., Artistic Director
  October 31, 2008

Teatro Izcalli

The mission of IZCALLI is to transform the lives of Chicano/a and Indigenous communities by promoting cultural consciousness, through the arts, historical education, and community dialogue.

IZCALLI

Izcalli, the Nahuatl word for "house of re-awakening," is a community-based organization that was founded in 1993 by a group of young Chicana/o activists in San Diego who wanted to create a space for young Chicana/o students to learn about their history and culture. As an all volunteer organization, Izcalli established a Saturday school program known as the Escuelita and began working with kindergarten-aged children to young adults. The curriculum ranged from the Aztec calendar to graffiti art. The Escuelita has since evolved and is now Proyecto Ollin, a summer project for 6 weeks on Saturdays that is free to students. In 1995, Teatro Izcalli was created, a comedy troupe that addresses the issues, challenges, and traditions of Chicanos/Latinos. Teatro Izcalli has now grown into a respected theater group that tours the country and has produced two full-length original plays, Nopal Boy and Juan More Beer along with numerous actos (sketches) over the years, all of which have received acclaim and recognition.

Izcalli's intervention and youth development model centers on the Hombre Noble Program also known as the Circulo de Hombres (Circle of Men). Izcalli is a member of the National Compadres Network and works with Jerry Tello, who is well known for teaching this model. The Hombre Noble Program provides Latino young men; positive male role models, enriching cultural and recreational activities, and support to help them make positive choices, modify their behavior, and become more engaged in school. Additionally, for over 10 years Izcalli has hosted the Annual Mens Gathering in which youth and men of all ages come together to dialogue for 3 days in ceremony. Izcalli also offers Cihua Ollin, Nahuatl for "movement of women" for Latinas. Cihua Ollin uses the talking circle format to address issues that pertain to women as students, professionals, mothers, artists, wives, daughters, and leaders, by creating a space for support and well- being for Latinas of different generations.

Through all of its' programs, Izcalli has reached thousands of community members and has served hundreds of Latino youth, encouraging and helping them to stay and excel in school, go to college, and give back to their communities.

Teatro Izcalli

INTRODUCTION

It is a pleasure to write this introduction to Teatro Izcalli and Macedonio Arteaga's first anthology of actos. Since the inception of Teatro Izcalli in 1995, the Teatro members have been committed to educating and entertaining their audiences with theatre for social change. All of the plays, sketches and actos in this collection have been performed successfully due to the talented actors, musicians, designers and technicians the Teatro has worked with over the years. The Teatro has performed in a variety of venues all over California as well as in Arizona, Wisconsin and as far east as Columbia University, entertaining audiences from all walks of life. Teatro Izcalli is an important Teatro, reaching young and old, Latina/os and non-Latina/os as they expose the human foibles that make for insightful laughter. People have enjoyed these creative expressions of the hopes and dreams, frustrations and battles that they see reflected on the stage. Whether in an educational setting, a professional venue or in a community center, audiences have cheered the Teatro members. Thus, as you read these works, remember that they are meant to come alive on a stage or in a lecture hall—where ever the Teatro members have found themselves as they toured. Remember, also, that the acto is meant to be adjusted to the local setting. For example, the names of local politicians will be substituted in order to bring the message home. As a theatre historian, I believe it is important to place these works and the Teatro members themselves, in their historical context, for they have their roots in the earliest theatrical expressions of the *Mexicanas* and *Mexicanos*, Chicanas and Chicanos living in the United States.

As a colonized people living in what used to be Mexico, Chicanos have always found humor in their fractured, neo-colonial Southwestern existence. They've enjoyed making fun of themselves as well as ridiculing the invading Anglos' customs, manners and ideas. The tensions created within and between these disparate communities have created anxieties that have fueled the comedy of the Chicanos for generations--indeed, before they *were* Chicanos, which is to say, before what were the northern reaches of Mexico became the US Southwest in 1848.

When the Chicanos began organizing in the late 1960's, feeling marginalized and neglected by traditional notions of Western Civilization, and what was called "American history," they looked for their roots in an ancient, mythical Mexico, rather than Mount Olympus and a western European paradigm. They saw themselves as the descendants of Mexican revolutionaries, Pancho Villa and Emiliano Zapata, not George Washington or Thomas Jefferson. Studying Pre-Columbian history, the Chicanos' learned that the Aztecs' diaspora had taken them to what is now Mexico City in the mid-14th century, where they built the center of a tremendous empire. Further, the Aztecs had migrated from the north, a mythical place they called Aztlán. Seeing themselves as descendants of the Aztecs, the Chicanos' adopted the term, Aztlán, to indicate the Southwest.

If we follow that logic, that the Chicanos' roots are firmly planted in Aztlán, then we can understand when they say: "We did not come to the United States, the United States came to us." Or perhaps more stridently, "We didn't cross the border, the border crossed us!" Despite the border, there is a constant flow of immigrants from Mexico into the US, which has kept the Spanish language and Mexican cultural identities alive as well. This persistent exchange of cultural capital and labor has fueled the theatre of the Chicanos as they express their ethnic identities and marginal positions in both the US and Mexico. And although Chicanos could, conceivably go home to Mexico, I have yet to see a Chicano play about immigrating to Mexico. They see Aztlán as home. Yet, regardless of whether the Chicanos call the Southwest "Aztlán," it really is not home in the sense that they feel they belong there, either. How could they, when traditional history books ignore their very existence? Where the media eradicates their presence or, worse, casts them as stereotypical victims or victimizers?

The Chicana/os are generally considered to be descendants of early African, Spanish and Indian peoples who have lived in a kind of unified disunity since Cortez first landed on the shores of Veracruz, Mexico, in 1519. And even amidst the Teatro Izcalli slaughter perpetuated by the colonizers in the name of a Christian god, *the people knew how to laugh.* They had to. The indigenous people made fun of the Spaniards' customs, their pale skin, hairy bodies and faces, their body odor and their hypocrisies. And although the native people's voices were generally silenced, there is no doubt that there must have been some rousing re-creations of the "Gachupines' " human foibles and failings. Although we do not have accounts of any private performances, human nature tells us that the natives, like the African slaves that would soon follow, found ways to make fun of their masters—*when the masters were not looking.*

Like any other ethnic group, Chicanos have responded to their marginalization with laughter to build community, uniting in a common cause. I believe that they have employed humor in their theatre as a means of protection, as a weapon and as an educational tool. Chicanos laugh at the weaknesses of their oppressors and in so doing, feel superior to them. Indeed, nothing could be funnier to the oppressed than to make fun of the oppressor, to bring him down to size. As we all know, laughter is a very powerful expression, allowing the marginalized and oppressed to find her voice in ridiculing the "master" and other adversaries, if only for a moment.[1] Adding to their sense of otherness, Chicanos have often performed their comedies outside the mainstream, on the margins, effectively in private.

In like manner, laughter has also been used as a weapon by the oppressors. As Albert Memmi, in *The Colonizer and the Colonized*, observed, it is incumbent upon the colonizer to make the colonized feel inferior. Besides destroying anything that gives the subaltern a sense of culture, place and agency, the colonizer must do all that he can to erase the colonial subject's identity. However, the Chicanos, like their indigenous ancestors, recognized this post-colonial project early on and turned the colonizers gaze back upon his own absurdities and failings.

For some observers, Chicano theatre has its more direct roots in Mexican tent shows, called "carpas." From the 1920's into the middle of the 20th century, carpas, so named for the tents in which they performed, toured all across Mexico and the Southwestern U.S. Aimed at the working classes, the carpas were variety shows, like vaudeville, in which audiences were treated to songs, dances, and other acts as well as sketches that resonated with the Mexicans who found themselves in an alien environment. Popular figures such as the *pelado* and *pelada* made audiences laugh with their comic shtick and topical themes. The legendary Mexican comic actor, Mario Moreno, began his career in the carpas, where

[1][NOTE: Also, according to Dana F. Sutton, comedy can produce a catharsis. The Catharsis of Comedy, Lanham: Rowman & Littlefield, 1994.]

he created his famous pelado, Cantinflas, the little guy who comes through against all odds resisting a variety of villains and obstacles.

El Teatro Campesino And Other Teatros

In 1965, Luis Valdez and a group of striking farm workers founded the Teatro Campesino as a performing arm of the incipient farm workers' union being organized by the late Cesar Chavez and Dolores Huerta. Under Valdez's direction the farm workers collectively created what he termed actos, direct descendants of the carpa sketches. When the Teatro Campesino began touring to colleges and universities in 1967, the troupe effectively dropped seeds of creativity wherever they performed. Chicana and Chicano students who witnessed the Teatro's actos said to themselves, "We can do that." And they did, collectively creating their own actos based on their struggles: as students in an alien environment; as activists committed to social change on campus and in their communities. Teatro Izcalli is a direct descendant of the Teatro Campesino and the early Chicano theatre groups that soon followed.

One of the most enduring performance groups that also owes its inception to the Teatro Campesino is the world-famous trio, Culture Clash. It is important to note that the members of Teatro Izcalli have also been influenced in their creative processes by this trio. Founded in San Francisco in the mid-1980s as Comedy Fiesta, the members of the original group, were the late Jose Antonio Burciaga, Marga Gomez, Richard Montoya, Monica Palacios, Ric Salinas and Herbert Siguenza. Eventually, the group became a trio comprised (to this day) of Montoya, Salinas and Siguenza, who have gone on to national significance through their 25+ years of performing in a variety of genres. Indeed, like the Teatro Campesino, other comedy troupes were inspired by Culture Clash including Berkeley's Chicano Secret Service and Los Angeles-based Mal Ojo. Unlike the members of most community-based teatros like Izcalli, the members of Culture Clash perform full-time, earning a living with their productions. But the founding members of Teatro Izcalli were either still in college or recent graduates of local San Diego colleges and universities; professionals whose commitment to social justice was expressed through their creative efforts. Today, the members of Teatro Izcalli hold full-time jobs, juggling their busy calendars and commitments in order to

`Teatro Izcalli`

continue their tours and performances.

This compilation is the result of thirteen years of collaboration between Macedonio Arteaga and the Teatro members in the tradition of earlier carpas and teatros. The first piece in this collection is Arteaga's *Nopal Boy*, one of the Teatro's most successful and longest-running plays.[2] Like so many previous actos, plays and carpa sketches, *Nopal Boy* critiques the "vendido" type, the Chicano or Mexican who refuses to acknowledge his or her culture. In this case, it is a young man, Marcos, who discovers a nopal, or cactus, growing out of his forehead. Nobody else sees it but him and the humor this situation causes is palpable with any Mechicana/o audience. The initiated know that when someone whose coloring and facial features show clearly indigenous influences, says "I'm not Mexican," observers will say to themselves, "*Pues, ¡tiene el nopal en la frente!*" ("Well, he has a cactus on his forehead!"). In other words, "Who does he think he's fooling?"

When *Nopal Boy* was first produced, the settings were designed by the world-famous San Diego artist, Victor Ochoa. Marcos's journey includes archetypal figures, such as the Devil himself, disguised as a variety of characters, recalling the Spanish religious folk plays of the Colonial period. Ultimately, *Nopal Boy* is about cultural redemption, a demonstration of the joy of recognizing one's Mexican heritage. It takes a journey back to Marcos' grandmother's home in *Mexico* to reveal his Truth as a Mexican. It is a comic and telling piece that plays upon the audiences' knowledge of the types being satirized.

El Nopal Boy is followed by a number of actos, some very brief, like "blackouts," others longer, that all reveal the varieties of experiences the Teatro members and the director/playwright, Arteaga, have experienced and which demonstrate their critique of society. It is to the group's credit that they critique the Chicano Movement itself in such actos as "Chicano Rehab," in which they ridicule various stereotypes of Chicano activists. From the super-feminist to the paranoid "veterano," the characters in this acto evoke types familiar to any Chicana/o activist and if they can laugh at themselves, perhaps they might take away some wisdom.

Each of the actos in this collection has been performed successfully and I urge the reader to imagine these creative

---

[2] I am honored to say that Macedonio was my student when he first wrote the acto and I enjoyed it so much that I urged him to keep working on it for a possible production by the then developing Teatro.

pieces *performed* in front of an audience of Raza, people who can relate to the images being represented. The actos are all bilingual, an important part of the premise of Teatro Chicano, for the combination of Spanish, English and even caló, give the Mechicana/o audience members a feeling of superiority because they can understand the language. Ultimately, even the non-bilingual audience member can understand the dialogue because of the situations being portrayed and because of the total picture. But the total picture belongs to the Mechicana/os living their fractured existence in what was Aztlán. So enjoy these delightful, insightful pieces, cognizant of the fact that they did not come out of a vacuum, full-blown, but are a part of the Mechicana/os history.

Jorge Huerta, Ph.D.
University of California San Diego

Teatro Izcalli

JORGE HUERTA, Ph.D.

Prof. Huerta is a Chancellor's Associates Professor of Theatre at the University of California, San Diego, where he began teaching in the department of Theatre and Dance in 1975. He has directed in regional theatres throughout the United States and taken two student groups to perform in Spain, France and Germany. Huerta is also a leading authority on contemporary Chicana/o and US Latina/o theatre who has lectured throughout the US, Latin America and Western Europe. He has published many articles and reviews in journals and anthologies and has edited three collections of plays. Prof. Huerta published the first book about Chicano theatre, Chicano Theatre: Themes and Forms in 1982. Dr. Huerta was inducted into the College of Fellows of the American Theatre in 1994 and elected National Association of Chicana and Chicano Studies, (NACCS) Scholar, in 1997. He was honored with the Domingo Ulloa Cultural Award by the California Rural Legal Assistance in 2005. Huerta's latest book, Chicano Drama: Society, Performance and Myth, was published by Cambridge University Press in late 2000. From 2005 through 2007 Chancellor Marye Anne Fox appointed Dr. Huerta to the position of Associate Chancellor and Chief Diversity Officer for UC San Diego. In 2007 Huerta was awarded the Association for Theatre in Higher Education (ATHE) "Lifetime Achievement in Educational Theatre Award." In 2008 he was recognized as the "Distinguished Scholar" by the American Society for Theatre Research (ASTR), the Society's highest annual honor. Dr. Huerta has been married to Ginger Huerta for 43 years. They have two sons, Ronald, married to Ariane Compagnon Huerta and Gregory.

Teatro Izcalli

In 2005, Ashley Lucas conducted an interview with
Teatro Izcalli. At the time, Ms. Lucas was a Ph.D.
student at UCSD and her dissertation was on Chicano
theatre. This is the interview that she facilitated with
several members of the group.

A MOMENT WITH TEATRO IZCALLI
ASHLEY LUCAS

A Moment With Teatro Izcalli: Macedonio Arteaga,
Alicia Chavez, Iyari Arteaga, and Claudia Cuevas.
Conducted by Ashley Lucas
San Diego, California
December 2, 2005

LUCAS: For the record, state your names and when you joined the group.
ALICIA: Alicia, founding member.
IYARI: My name's Iyari, and I guess founding member.
CLAUDIA: Claudia Cuevas, eight years ago.
MACEDONIO: Macedonio Arteaga, founding member of Teatro Izcalli.
LUCAS: How did the group get started?
ALICIA: Basically, Izcalli was a Saturday school program that started in
1993. For two years we were doing the *escuelita*, and then Mace had this
idea to start a theatre group, a comedy troupe. We would use the funds
raised by the comedy troupe to go back into the *escuelita*. In June of
1995, it was the first year of the Chicano Youth Leadership Camp, and
they approached us because they'd heard we were thinking about starting a
teatro group. They asked us if we wanted to perform, and it was our first
official gig. It just kind of happened. Those of us who were in Izcalli,

13

were already involved with the *escuelita* when we came together to do this.

LUCAS: Claudia, you've talked before about how you had been in M.E.Ch.A., and that's how you got involved in Izcalli. But what did you think of the *teatro* group when you first saw them? What made you want to get involved?

CLAUDIA: The message, the message that they were doing. I saw how high school students were reacting to them and I had never seen Chicano theatre. I grew up half the time in Mexico, half the time here, and I had never seen anybody tell my story. Growing up in the United States as a Mexican American and then becoming a Chicana, I didn't know who Cesar Chavez was. I didn't know any of that when I was in elementary [school], and I think the first skit I saw them perform was "Escuelita." I was in awe. They were funny, I thought, "I've always wanted to be an actress!" When the opportunity came—as petrified as I was—I jumped at the opportunity to perform because I wasn't going to be famous. I wasn't going to be a real actress, but I wanted to do something that was educational. Being a Chicana, that was the most important thing for me. It was a really great opportunity.

MACEDONIO: It is *real drama*. (*Everyone laughs.*)

LUCAS: Well, I think it's important to recognize that what you do is real theatre. Just because you're not in repertory at the San Diego Rep or something like that doesn't mean that what y'all do isn't real performance. It's engaging the community in real ways.

ALICIA: Yes, I think that's been an evolution amongst our selves. Personally, I didn't consider myself as an actress. In the beginning, I was just doing it for the cause, for Izcalli, for the kids, and then as the years went by, we started developing more skill and more—developing our craft, as they say. (*Laughs.*) I really started feeling like, "Hey, you know, I really am an artist!" That's my evolution.

CLAUDIA: I always thought, "I'm funny." I can make people laugh from being silly and I'm an educator. That's how I always see it because, you know, we're not method actors.

MACEDONIO: I know we're method actors! (*Everyone laughs.*)

MACEDONIO: You know what's funny? When we performed with Culture Clash in—what, ninety. . .

ALICIA: That was in '98.

MACEDONIO: '98?

ALICIA: '98, 'cause I was on the board at the Centro.

Teatro Izcalli MACEDONIO: Well, we did a show with Culture Clash, and they obviously saw us perform. I don't know if they meant it—It doesn't matter. They could be lying, but they said, "This is the premiere Chicano comedy troupe in the United States."

14

ALICIA: No, they said San Diego! (*Laughs.*)

MACEDONIO: Really? (*Everyone laughs.*) Well, then *we are* the premiere Chicano comedy troupe in San Diego because we're the only one! (*Everyone laughs.*)

ALICIA: I think he said San Diego.

MACEDONIO: Naw, he didn't say San Diego.

ALICIA: Okay, okay.

MACEDONIO: We never thought about our selves like that. It was just like, we're just having fun. When they said that—whether they meant it or didn't mean it, it doesn't matter. It was like, "Hey, we kind of are doing something that's cool." Yeah, we're just kind of following what they're doing, but to have people really acknowledge the stuff you have accomplished. We've literally been offered grants—like we didn't look for them! People literally *came to us.* The two big grants we've gotten, they were literally given to us. Somebody saw our show and said, "You know what? We want to give you $30,000 to do something on the census." And then the work that we did teaching theatre to little kids in San Ysidro, they came. They told me, "You know what? Apply for this. We want you guys to teach theatre to kids." So, it's like when you first starting writing as a poet, you write stuff that you don't want no one to see 'cause it's like your feelings or whatever. But then finally someone reads it, and somebody else reads it. Then people want to publish it, and then, "Whoa! Whoa!" You start believing in yourself more. We all struggle with that feeling of, "Well, we're not real actors." You know what I mean? Real actors know anthologies and whatever, that just made no sense but you know we don't know any of that stuff!

LUCAS: But I think it's important to acknowledge that you guys *are* doing theatre. Theatre is not just a high class thing. Theatre is not just for wealthy people. Theatre is not just for white people. Theatre is not just for people who have the time, money, and luxury of sitting in a dark theatre and paying for it. It's for everybody, and we've always understood that about poetry and visual art and so many other creative media, about books and things.

MACEDONIO: But not theatre.

LUCAS: But not theatre. We think that you have to be high class in order to do it, and that is just not true. You guys are doing theatre as much as Culture Clash is doing it when they're performing in these big fancy places. You're doing theatre as much as anybody who's doing Shakespeare somewhere, and that's what's interesting about what you do because you're engaging communities.

CLAUDIA: Theatre in Europe used to be done in open air and in the plazas, and people would throw things. You had to be careful if you

15

weren't good!

MACEDONIO: Así es en México también. En México they have hundreds of people who go watch. . .

ALICIA: Teatro is everywhere.

MACEDONIO: Yeah, but in this country it's like. . .

ALICIA: . . .an elitist thing. But that's very true what you said, and I just think about the kids who are associated with our family—of course, Iyari but like our nieces and nephews and people in Izcalli, like their kids—they've all grown up seeing us, seeing *teatro*. So they're not growing up with that idea, how we used to see it, that *teatro* isn't something for them. So they're seeing it as a part of them. They see themselves performing, and that whole elitist vision has been obliterated. I think of Iyari and how she's grown up totally, completely different from how I did. She's been involved in the teatro group since the beginning.

MACEDONIO: I never saw theatre, period.

ALICIA: Yeah.

MACEDONIO: So I didn't know it.

ALICIA: Yeah, so many Chicanitos. . .

MACEDONIO: . . .didn't know what the hell it was.

ALICIA: It's awful.

CLAUDIA: The community centers and schools where they present theatre, they don't charge. We don't charge. We ask for a donation, if possible, but that's so important. That's the only way we do it.

MACEDONIO: We charged for this last one.

CLAUDIA: We did? I thought we asked for a donation.

MACEDONIO: Yeah.

CLAUDIA: Okay, sorry. $10.

LUCAS: It's important, I think, to do theatre work that way, and I'd be interested to hear you all talk more about how you see your selves engaging the community. You've talked about your children and your family, but the people that you're not related to—why these people? Why are you connecting with the audiences that you have sought out by performing in the places where you do?

MACEDONIO: The big reason is that we do the leg work to fill our audiences. We work with a lot of these students through the summer program that we have, through the leadership camp that we have. We're helping our selves by building our own audience. You know what I mean?

ALICIA: Are you asking us why. . .

Teatro Izcalli MACEDONIO: I thought she meant how. . .

CLAUDIA: I'll give you an example. We have one of our *actos* called "*Educación Más Alta*," and we present it to a lot of different organizations. The kids who are college bound or not

16

college bound relate because they can relate to the girl trying to get to college. Then the characters of the mom and the dad, the girl's parents, are characters that they really relate to because they really feel that we capture the way that they would react. The things that we say are very much Mexican. Those are things that you see in a Mexican home, not in a Mexican American home, but a Mexican home. So now the parents can relate—the first generation—because that's how their mom talked to them, or that's exactly how they're talking to their child. So that's how my mom talked to me—and my dad—so that's the whole connection. It is the Chicano part of it, but it's also very much Mexican. Across the board, they see themselves in one or another character, so it's like, "Oh, that was funny! I may not have laughed on the cholo one or the spray paint guy, but when the dad came out and—'¿Hijo, de que estás hablando?'—oh, I know who that is. That's me, or that's my grandfather, or that's my great-grandfather." That's why I think people relate and come back and want to bring other people.

LUCAS: Right. You've mentioned several times the message of the group. If you had to condense it—any of you—into one or two sentences, what is the message of Teatro Izcalli?

MACEDONIO: When we all perform, Ashley, everybody out there on stage is a college graduate. So we show the students in the audience that they to can graduate. That's a huge message for the young people. We go into communities where kids have never seen theatre before, and the place is packed. After the show all the actors say "We all graduated from college." You know that the majority of these kids don't have that many role models that they can look up to in their neighborhood and say, "Wow! Oh my God! Look at this! I'm looking at three females and three males that graduated from college, and they're telling stories about my mom and my dad and my family at home." Where else are they going to see something like that? Where else are they going to get a chance to laugh at them selves? That's a huge message we're getting outside of our actos.

CLAUDIA: It's okay. It's okay. We can laugh at our lives.

ALICIA: Yeah.

CLAUDIA: We can laugh at our lives, and it's on stage. And it's okay because that's life.

ALICIA: But that's the message, and it's so healing just to laugh.

LUCAS: What do you guys see the group doing five or ten years from now? What is it that you want for Izcalli?

ALICIA: I think Mace should answer that.

MACEDONIO: A musical.

ALICIA: (Laughing.) A musical! We had plans to do a musical.

17

CLAUDIA: No, we didn't.

MACEDONIO: And I might tell you, I don't know how to write that.

ALICIA: We were going to write one.

LUCAS: What was it?

ALICIA: When we went to New York, we went to Columbia University. . .

MACEDONIO: Oh, don't even talk about it. (*Everyone laughs.*)

ALICIA: Who came up with the idea? I think Michelle came up with the idea? Or Claudia?

CLAUDIA: (*Emphatically.*) No.

ALICIA: I think it was Claudia.

CLAUDIA: (*Laughing.*) No!

ALICIA: Well, we were talking about musicals, and they came up with the brilliant idea of us starting the show with singing "New York, New York." (*Laughs.*)

MACEDONIO: That was funny. Let me just say something. She's missing a big part of this.

ALICIA: I've blocked it out. I don't remember it.

MACEDONIO: Everybody was like, "You need to write more stuff. We don't have enough material." I was like, "Shit, I don't got time to write!" And everybody yelled at me because there was no new material, so I said, "All right. Fine. You guys write whatever the hell you want." They wrote this stuff, and I was like, "Aw!" (Everyone laughs.)

CLAUDIA: Now you remember why we don't write.

ALICIA: I wasn't part of that writing team!

MACEDONIO: It was bad! I just went along with it because I'm trying to learn and grow. . .

CLAUDIA: That was the first and last time we wrote.

ALICIA: What was it? I don't even remember it.

CLAUDIA: It was just bad. Here's the thing. The Izcalli when I first joined it would take a mainstream theme movie or something and then make it Chicano. Like "Bosque Gump" and all those things.

MACEDONIO: Not all the *actos* were like that.

CLAUDIA: No, no, no. But that was one of the themes or styles that we—like, what would happen if we put a Mexican in that role, and let's see what would happen. So, I'm always saying things like, "Let's make *Grease* into *Chicano Grease*!" and we were going to do. . .

ALICIA: ¡*Grasa*! (*Laughs.*)

Teatro Izcalli

CLAUDIA: What was the one that we were talking about doing on Dances with Wolves, but it was Dances with. . .

ALICIA: *Cholos*!

MACEDONIO: Aw!

ALICIA: We've had a lot of ideas.

MACEDONIO: Real stupid ones.

ALICIA: Yeah.

CLAUDIA: So it was like, yeah, "New York, New York," and it wasn't funny. People were just like with their mouths open, going, "What are they doing?"

ALICIA: So that's why we haven't done a musical. We're sticking to the comedy basically.

MACEDONIO: Getting back to your question as to where I see Izcalli in the future, I definitely would like to see our work published and to see students—not only here in San Diego but in the Southwest, even outside the Southwest—performing our *actos*. Having teachers use it as a curriculum for kids to learn to read, for them to engage in their own history and their culture. To be seen like Luis Valdez's *actos*. They fit very well, even today, with simple performances. The community has changed. This isn't a farm-working community like it was at one time. It has changed, so the issues have changed. I don't want to sound arrogant or whatever, but I think our group has captured what Luis Valdez did in the fields. What he did in the fields, we've captured here in our own community, which is pretty much a lot of communities throughout the United States now that are in urban settings. I would love to see that grow and be able to have our work published and other people use it, and eventually having our own space. We teach kids theatre in the summer, and we have a leadership camp where kids learn more about this. We're doing it. I think we're halfway there, probably way more than halfway because having these actos published is going to be a big thing because it legitimizes the work.

IYARI: What about like a new generation of Teatro Izcalli or something? Like when you guys don't want to act anymore, you know what I mean? Do you want it to die out, or for younger people to come and take over?

MACEDONIO: Of course we do not want it die out. We are passing it on, it's already happening. We have Mike. We have Greñas.

ALICIA: Yes, that's definitely what I want. For it to continue for the next generation, maybe Iyari and her peers to continue with the production of things, maybe with us dinosaurs in the background. That's the vision that I have.

CLAUDIA: I'd like to see us do something like what Culture Clash did with A *Bowl of Beings*, where now that's being used in classrooms. The core people are the ones that did it, and then from there it goes off, other people performing it, doing it, evolving it. I think it's important to have something visual because we're not in the same type of generation where print was important unfortunately. Visual is the new generation, and it's important to have something that people can see.

ALICIA: We've been talking about producing a video, and then it was a movie, then a video. It's taken on several different transformations, so I don't know what stage we're at right now. That's definitely something that we'd like to have and bringing in some of the old people that were part of the group. Because there are some characters that are so much that of the actor, like Benny as he portrayed Bosque Gump. There's no one else in the group that can do it like he did it, having that on film, having that on video. Then we'd have something that could be part of the book. That way when a school purchases the book, they'd have the video.

LUCAS: Is there anything else that you all want people to know about Teatro Izcalli?

ALICIA: I think what drives us to do the work we do. It's the love not only for the art form but the love for the community also. I'm reaching people, touching people in this way. It's all on a volunteer basis. We do it because we love it, because it's within us to—obviously we're Chicanas and Chicanos—but we feel it's important to relay the messages.

IYARI: Like she said, we don't get much doing this, but we get a better reward, like people being happy.

CLAUDIA: That's it. I was sick, and Mace, was like, "Can you still do this?" And I was like, "I *need* to do it." The energy that you get performing in front of other people when you feel like they got it—Wow! It helped me through a lot. It was one of the best things for my energy because people were laughing. They were laughing not *at* me but with me.

MACEDONIO: I love history, and I'm a historian, I guess. I think one of the things about our group is that we don't really realize what we're doing because we're just doing it. I literally get emails from people, and they say, "Oh, this is awesome. I've never seen anything like it." And these are people we don't even know. They emailed me thanking me. You don't realize the impact you're having on people because you're just doing it because you feel you have to do it. That's what's really awesome. I've gotten emails or phone calls where I've been able to carry out a dream. It's what happened to me when I saw Culture Clash. Now when people see us, I know there's been a lot of Macedonio's in the audience who were just blown away, mesmerized. Not necessarily because we're awesome performers, but because we're communicating their voice on stage. And they're laughing. I've spoken at college classes were

Teatro Izcalli

kids are staring at me the whole time, and afterwards, I'm like, "Hey, what's up?" And they come up to me and say, "I saw you when I was in sixth grade, and I still remember your play. It changed my life." It's like dang! I want to start crying. It's like

20

wow! You don't realize what you do because you're just doing it. That's really the real thing is seeing the Chicano and Chicana youth. You're here to make a difference, and you see what our people are going through. We're losing them. We're losing the war here. We're not succeeding in college. We're not making it anywhere. If we can make a little bit of a difference in somebody's life—this guy I talked to yesterday who works for the Environmental Coalition—He's the director. He said, "I took my whole family to your last show, and we talk about something in your skit every single day." They went camping, and they saw a hawk. And they all started laughing, and they were all laughing because of how I go— (*makes a little whistling noise*)—when I play that guy [in the "Chicano Rehab" *acto*]. And he says the whole family, the wife, the kids—they all did the same thing, and they were laughing. You don't think that you're impacting people like that because you're just doing it. It's silly. I made that up. I've never done that before. I just made it up on stage. And the guy said, "Oh, that was great, man! That was hilarious, and my kids— they'd never seen it before, and they keep asking me, 'When will we see it again?' and 'Do they have a video?'" And I've gotten emails from people telling me, "Can you send me a video?" And it's like, "Well, we don't have a video. We're working on it." The thing is, we don't think of our selves like that. We're just having fun. You know, the fan mail. . .

ALICIA: (*Laughing.*) Oh, shut up!

CLAUDIA: People have been asking me, "When are you going to Hollywood?" And I'm like, "Huh? Uh, no." First of all, 'cause I'm like, "No." And then second of all because that has no purpose. I don't feel like that would make sense for me. I like what we do. I wish we could get famous at what we do, (*Everyone laughs.*) but I like what we do.

ALICIA: We've had a lot of opportunities to travel, and we've met a lot of people.

LUCAS: You all travel as a group, but your home base is San Diego. Your work is so largely about San Diego. Your project is very different than, say, a Culture Clash which goes from town to town. A lot of groups that do *acto*-format kind of humor end up traveling and doing that instead of staying attached to a community for a whole decade. That's quite an accomplishment.

ALICIA: (*Laughing.*) We're great! Tell us more about us!

(*Everyone laughs.*)

MACEDONIO: Tell us more of what the hell we do!

ALICIA: When you said that, the first thing that popped into my head was "Mariabertos." Have you seen that skit? "Mariabertos"? I remember years ago we did it in L.A., and everybody was like, "Huh?" (*Everyone laughs.*) They just didn't get it 'cause here there's Roberto's, Alberto's,

21

Umberto's, da da da da da. In San Diego everybody gets it.

CLAUDIA: We're like a Mecca. We're a border town. We're right next to Mexico, there's new people coming in all the time. You're so there. You're right there.

MACEDONIO: Well, how would it be when you're sixty years old, and Teatro Izcalli's still around? Obviously not us.

ALICIA: You probably will be.

MACEDONIO: That's what my dream is, that it continues. I don't see this country changing in like forty, fifty years, so the need for Chicano theatre will still be here. We don't know. Maybe it's going to be more of a need. *No sabemos. ¿Verdad?*

LUCAS: I think good theatre is always addressing, in one form or another, the politics of what's happening in the community in the audience. You guys are really good about that. Not in having the inside jokes, like in "Mariaberto's," but in having a good grip on the pulse of your audience. Because you're not famous, you live in these communities you really are your selves. You didn't just come here and say, "Let me look at these people and do something." You grew up in these communities and are still talking to them and still living here. You're not trying to assimilate and climb the capitalist ladder and go somewhere else.

CLAUDIA: That's because nobody would provide our paycheck to make sense of our selves. That's part of it.

ALICIA: What's also important is that our group has always maintained— there's been several people who've been part of the group who've come and gone, and then we've also maintained this kind of open door policy to have guest performers. I think that's something that's unique to the group.

CLAUDIA: We pull in people from the audience, and I think that it's important that people see that when they're walking down the campus, "Hey that's the guy they pulled up and it was cool." We're all here, and anybody can do what we do.

ALICIA: We are accessible. We go to the community. We perform in Barrio Logan, Barrio Sherman, and all those other places where people in the community, *señoras* in the community—There's no way they're going to be able to go to the Rep. or the La Jolla Playhouse or whatever. We go out there to the *comunidad*. We're exposing our selves to everybody. (*Laughs.*) I don't know if that's the right word. (*Everyone laughs.*)

MACEDONIO: I expose myself every day. I'm just so worried about what pictures will get printed in the newspaper, man, with my big *lonja* coming out. . .

Teatro Izcalli

(*Everyone laughs.*)

ALICIA: Anyway!

22

MACEDONIO: We're going out to dinner, Ashley, if you want to go with us. . .

(*End of interview.*)

Teatro Izcalli

On December 11, 2005 the San Diego Union Tribune published an article featuring Chicano/Latino theatre groups including Teatro Izcalli. The article was titled "Missing in Action" and it focused on how Chicano/Latinos are now the majority but our voice on the theatrical stage still remains in the minority. This article reinforces the reason why we started doing Chicano theatre and why we felt the need to publish our own work.

MISSING IN ACTION
ANNE MARIE WELSH

It's a paradox: Even as the local Hispanic population grows, the number of Latino-themed plays here has shrunk

By Anne Marie Welsh
Theater Critic
December 11, 2005

Along with the "Grinch" and Scrooge and the "Nutcracker," the holidays bring "La Pastorela." In various forms, this traditional Mexican folk drama often appears on stages that do not showcase Latino voices during the rest of the year.

Some young Chicanos wouldn't be caught dead at even a hip pastorela like Teatro Mascara Magica's "La Pastorela Noel" at the Old Globe, yet bilingual families flock to these warmhearted annual events, a mix of nativity pageant and raucous comedy.

A survey of audiences, playwrights and theater institutions would find that the Latino theater scene is in flux. Yet one large irony cuts across the landscape:

As the proportion of the region's population that self-identifies as Hispanic (there is no Latino category in the U.S. Census) rises, the percentage of Latino-themed plays on the region's stages has shrunk.

The three largest regional theaters in Southern California – the Mark Taper Forum, South Coast Repertory and the Old Globe – have all cut out their specifically Latino play development initiatives, a move that drew heated controversy to L.A.'s Taper last spring.

Playwright Luis Alfaro and *New York Times* critic Margo Jefferson slammed the decision by new Taper head Michael Ritchie. But UCSD theater scholar Jorge Huerta calls such development programs "the projects" and suggests that the wealth of Latino playwrights now writing may no longer need to be ghettoized as they transition to the mainstream.

And while the Old Globe no longer reads and develops Latino plays through its Teatro Meta initiative, it has ramped up its educational activities among San Diego's diverse populations as an investment in future audiences. "We may not do such an extraordinary binational project as (the recent border-crossing) 'Romeo y Julieta'," said Globe executive Louis Spisto, "but we have two plays for students that will tour and our outreach into the schools continues."

The main purveyors of Latino work in San Diego County are the San Diego Repertory, which emphasizes Chicano and Latin-American traditions; La Jolla Playhouse, which has produced a less obvious, but steady stream of playwrights including Jose Rivera, Culture Clash and others; and Deborah Salzer's Playwrights Project, which discovered writer Josefina "Real Women Have Curves" Lopez among other young Latinos and Latinas.

Sam Woodhouse, founding artistic director of the San Diego Rep and an Anglo from Coronado, produces more Chicano and Latin American work than any theater manager locally. He's premiered three recent plays by the father of Chicano theater, Luis Valdez, among many others. Knowing that non-Hispanic whites will soon be a minority here, Woodhouse feels that theater should offer an encounter with the other. "I look in the mirror and see myself everyday," he said. "What I want to see on stage is someone who may not be like me."

He argues that there's nothing revolutionary about his theater's consciously multiethnic programming. "Go to your HMO and you'll see the ethnic mix that's there. This is not to be a do-gooder. It's not a food stamp program. It's about being honest. Diversity gives us strength." His mantra: "People really are interested in seeing plays about the place we call home."

Teatro Izcalli   Era of the projects

The topic of opportunities for Latinos in theater is a touchy one in a state in which a black man on the University of California Board of Regents, Ward Connelly, led the fight to end affirmative action in admissions. Yet at UCSD, despite the demise of such "entitlement" programs, Chicano scholar and stage director Huerta has been named associate chancellor and chief diversity officer.

"I call the days of foundation and government-funded Latino initiatives 'the era of the projects,' " says Huerta, a co-founder of Teatro Mascara Magica, which co-produces the Globe "Pastorela."

"A great deal of money from the Ford Foundation and the Lila Wallace/Readers' Digest Fund went to Anglo theaters for Latino playwrights, programming and other initiatives. A lot of plays were written and published at theaters who paid only a kind of lip service to Latino work."

Not only have those private funding initiatives so popular in the 1980s ended, but also the cutbacks and restructuring of grant categories at the National Endowment for the Arts and the death of California Arts Council grants have had a big impact.

Only theaters that have a "real, ongoing commitment to producing Latino work are going to do it now," Huerta said. He does not feel that regional theaters like the Old Globe or the Taper have any moral or artistic obligation to select plays that reflect the demographics of the region. "Why should they struggle to build a new audience if they've already cultivated their own without developing or producing Latino work? Why risk it?"

Woodhouse believes the Rep long ago answered any questions about whether mainstream (meaning white) theaters can sell tickets across ethnicities to a Latino play. "Of course you can, we proved that," says Woodhouse, pointing to the Valdez classic "Zoot Suit," based on the racial profiling that followed a notorious Los Angeles murder. "This was entertaining but not escapist fare and it was one of the biggest sellers in our 30 years."

Ticking off a recent list of well-attended Chicano and Latino works, he also named Valdez's poetic "The Mummified Deer" and "Nuevo California" by Bernardo Solano and Allan Havis about the first Mexican pope in a borderless region.

Woodhouse says "only a tiny handful" of non-Hispanic "subscribers ever say 'you've done too many Latino plays.' I am really proud of this commitment."

Grass-roots populism

Although Woodhouse, Huerta and Shirley Fishman, La Jolla Playhouse's associate artistic director, all caution that it's impossible to characterize the voices of Latino playwrights without being reductive, there are two large strains running through the history of Latino theater in the United States. One tends to the populist and comic and is rooted in the agitprop of Valdez and traditions of Mexican vaudeville. The other from more elite artistic and theatrical traditions of Spain and Latin America

Many voices have emerged from the Chicano theater movement of the 1960s, spawned by Valdez whose politically-charged actos accompanied the rise of Cesar Chavez and the United Farm Workers. From these short political plays performed on the backs of trucks in the fields came Teatro Campesino in 1965.

Some groups, including Culture Clash and several small San Diego theaters, have followed its lead, performing at first for their own communities and only later, if ever, moving into larger, more mainstream theaters such as the Rep.

Culture Clash itself demonstrates the impossibility of pigeonholing Latino theater artists. One member of the famed comedy trio that started in the 1980s, Richard Montoya, doesn't speak Spanish; the other two, Ric Salinas and Herbert Seguenza, are from Salvadoran backgrounds. Yet they're usually mislabeled Chicano, meaning politically active Mexican-Americans, and their heirs include grass-roots companies that present plays in Spanish or bilingually.

La Jolla Playhouse will co-produce Culture Clash's new "The Mask of Zorro" next season. Fishman says the project appealed to her staff not for any demographic reasons, but because it's an "examination of a Latino icon that does not have Latino origins. Zorro was an Irishman. So it's a perfect subject for Culture Clash since their work is all about cultural collisions and often, the politics of California."

Among San Diego's still-community-based theater projects are several in the Rep's Calafia Initiative and Macedonio Arteaga's Teatro Izcalli (which means seed, or literally "house of reawakening" in Nahuatl, a Mexican-Indian language).

Also in this populist tradition is a slicker, more television-influenced kind of sketch comedy. During the 1980s and early-to mid-1990s, shows by Latins Anonymous, monologuist Marga Gomez, and Rick Najera (a La Mesa-born actor-writer) found big cross-over audiences at several San Diego theaters. Najera's characters, including the redneck immigration agent Buford Gomez, have moved from San Diego to Broadway (where Najera's "Latinologues" opened last month and is still struggling to find an audience at the Helen Hayes Theatre).

One grass-roots San Diego group is different: It

Teatro Izcalli specializes in Mexican-Jewish stories and humor. But after 19 years of performing in Spanish, even Teatro Punto y Coma this year found a bigger audience by presenting its shows in English.

28

Following traditions

Unlike the populist writers, a large group of Latino playwright's appeals to more educated tastes. They draw inspiration from traditions of playwriting and performance in Spain and the native countries of the writers' immigrant families.

Often commissioned by South Coast Rep and other regionals, Nilo Cruz, the first Latino to win a Pulitzer Prize for drama for his "Anna in the Tropics" two years ago, moved to the States from Cuba when he was 10 years old. Playhouse regular Jose Rivera comes from a Puerto Rican immigrant family in New York; Ariel Dorfman is Chilean. And there are hyphenates such as the oft-produced UCSD-trained Naomi Iizuka who is Japanese-Latino and the fine comic writer Lisa Loomer; both write only obliquely about their Latina heritages.

Perhaps the greatest and certainly the most influential of living Latina-American playwrights is Maria Irene Fornes, a Cuban emigre. She joined the burgeoning off-off-Broadway theater movement in the 1960s and, like colleagues Sam Shepard and Lanford Wilson, has stayed active and unpredictable since. Her work is deeply rooted in a feminist and Latin sensibility, though it is also visually acute, often experimental and, in its themes and feeling, universal. In terms of influence, if not emphases and style, she's the East Coast equivalent of Valdez on the West, a fountainhead for future generations.

Fornes founded the Playwriting Lab at Intar, the Hispanic theater company responsible for nurturing and also producing many contemporary playwrights. Fornes' collage techniques and unwavering devotion to creating original works for the theater have influenced playwrights as diverse as UCSD-trained Caridad Svitch, "Angels in America" author Tony Kushner and fellow Cuban-American Eduardo Machado, who now heads Intar as well as the graduate playwriting program at Columbia University.

Because her vision is both political and poetic, Fornes is seldom showcased at risk-averse regional theaters, a fate that has driven some of her heirs, such as Rivera and San Francisco's Octavio Solis, to write for Hollywood or television.

Some work straddles populist and high art traditions. At spaces like Sushi Performance and Visual Art and Centro Cultural de la Raza during "the project years," sophisticated performers such as Guillermo Gomez-Pena mixed traditions and performed for art world audiences, while at grass-roots venues like community centers, says Arteaga, "90-percent of the audiences still have never seen a theater performance."

Similar themes do recur across this big range of Latino writing:

the challenge of assimilation, gender relations and macho, privilege and power since the conquest. Arteaga's soon-to-be-published "El Nopal Boy" concerns a local teenager who, though he "looks like Montezuma," wants so badly to fit in at his American high school that he fights to deny his Mexican heritage. A cactus, visible only to himself, begins sprouting from his forehead.

In Lisa Loomer's artful exploration of assimilation, the much-produced "Living Out," an immigrant woman from El Salvador struggles to bring her elder son to Los Angeles where she cares for the younger child and also works as a nanny raising the child of a Santa Monica lawyer. The two working women are seen as in many ways parallel. But beneath the apparent joke that their differences mask their gender similarities, the play also reveals the lawyer's privilege as a white professional and a U.S. citizen.

Gaining access

Access to theater is a big issue in any predominantly Mexican-American neighborhood, say Arteaga and the Old Globe's Spisto. While the Playhouse and the Globe address the access-to-theater issue by investing in future Latino audiences with their touring shows in schools, the larger problem of Mexican-American access to the arts is being addressed by a cadre of Cal State San Marcos professors.

Saxophonist Merryl Goldberg runs Centre Artes, an arts-in-education program that reaches out to Latino kids, both in the university and in their schools. She's on the visual and performing arts faculty with several artists such as David Avalos and Deborah Small, who previously made Centro Cultural de la Raza such a vital center for Chicano art and performance.

Funding cutbacks, administrative shake-ups and controversy within the Chicano community pushed Balboa Park's Centro Cultural off the city's cultural map. "But the current board of directors who wanted to go more corporate is negotiating with the city and the Chicano community," says Arteaga whose Teatro used to be headquartered there. He remains hopeful the Centro will renew its mission and revitalize itself.

The interdependence of the newly arrived and the already assimilated in this region of immigrants suggests a rich theatrical vein few mainstream San Diego theaters are mining. North Coast Repertory, Lamb's Players, Cygnet, Moonlight and other venues seldom stage such work. And surprisingly there's still no major Latino

Teatro Izcalli theater here.

Arteaga, when he thinks about it, defines himself as a Mexican-Indian Chicano. He thinks many San Diego theaters are missing a good thing in not reaching the growing "Hispanic" population.

"This is our home," he says, "We've been here for a couple of thousand years. We're not going anyplace. We're potentially a very big audience."

Used with permission from San Diego Union Tribune, December 2005.

MISSING IN ACTION

Formerly headquartered at Centro Cultural de la Raza, Teatro Izcalli now operates from a charter school in Chula Vista; (from left) Teatro Izcalli's Jose Alvarez, founder Macedonio Arteaga, Alicia Chavez-Arteaga and Claudia Cuevas. *Dan Trevan / Union-Tribune*

Teatro Izcalli

I wrote Nopal Boy while I was in college as Jorge Huerta mentioned in the introduction of this book. Nopal Boy is symbolic of my personal journey of finding my identity and struggling with who I was as a Mexican immigrant. There's an old saying in the Mexican culture for those who try to deny their "Mexicaness". *Tiene el nopal en la frente.* Losely it means "don't try to pretend you're not Mexican with that cactus growing out of your forehead". I thought of that saying because no matter what, I could never get rid of that imaginary cactus growing out of my forehead. I had to accept I was Mexican and be proud of it. When we performed the play, it brought a lot of healing as well to some of the actors who also struggled with their own identity at one time. I hope you enjoy Nopal Boy and that you may have further discussions on the issue of identity.

NOPAL BOY
By Macedonio Arteaga Jr.

CHARACTERS:

FATHER - Around fifty years old. He works in landscaping. Father is very laid back and just goes along with everything his wife says.
DOCTOR DICENADA - A mad scientist type. He doesn't make sense most of the time but does have his own weird logic. He's wearing a doctor gown with boots and long hair.
MOM - A strong, forty-eight year old, Mexican woman who is very loud and runs the household. In the scenes at home, she wears an apron that has cacti (*nopales*) all over it.
GRANDMA - A powerful woman about seventy years old who knows about traditional medicine, she's known as a *curandera*. She has lived in Mexico her whole life. Even though her role is brief, she's a strong figure toward the end of the play. She's dressed **nopal boy** in a long dress (*huipil*).
MARCOS - About seventeen years old. He's extremely confused about his

identity. He doesn't really spend much time with his family until he makes a trip to Mexico. Marcos is embarrassed of being Mexican. He prefers to call himself Spanish. When Marcos speaks in Spanish he sounds like an Anglo speaking Spanish.

TAXI CAB DRIVER/COP/DEVIL - The Taxi Cab Driver is a crazy man that has supernatural powers (devil like) who can get anything, anytime, any place. The Cop is a very angry, crazy, negative and racist man.

ANGLO WOMAN - Anglo woman in her 20's and a "material girl" type.

FLIGHT ATTENDANT - A young woman in her 20's wearing a green suit with Nopal Alas on her skirt.

CANDY- A blonde 18 year old girl who's very happy and supportive of Marcos.

AURELIA ZUNIGA - A news reporter.

DUDE - An Anglo surfer with long blonde hair.

COMADRE 1 - A middle aged woman dressed in colorful clothing wearing lots of make-up.

COMADRE 2 - A middle aged woman wearing a reboso.

CHUNKY - A heavy set character with a big mustache and a mask covering his eyes.

(*The stage is set in the living room of Marcos' home. There are cactus all over the place but the people living in the house aren't bothered by the cactus and don't really see them.*)

SCENE ONE

(Mom *is dressed as a maid. Father is dressed as a gardener. A Vicente Fernández song is playing in the background.* Marcos is *sitting on a couch wearing a San Diego Chargers jersey. He has a lightning bolt painted on his cheek.*)

MARCOS: Come on *pinche* Chargers!! Damn, I hate rooting for this team. Why do I go for these guys anyway? Man, they suck! Turn that Mexican music down! (*Mumbling.*) I can't stand that Mexican music! (*When he says that, he gets an itch on his forehead, a sharp itch. He scratches it.*)

FATHER: (*Walks into the living room.*) ¿Mijo, que estás viendo?

MARCOS: *Futbol Americano, papí.*

FATHER: Why don't you watch soccer, *mijo? Las Chivas* and *America* are on. *Es el clásico.* (Father *grabs the remote and changes the channel. You hear a Mexican soccer game in the background.*)

MARCOS: Come on, dad. I don't want to watch that.

Teatro Izcalli

34

FATHER: (*Yelling at television.*) *¡Ay menso, tira con la izquierda! Es una vergüenza.* (Father *is into the game but* Marcos *is very upset because* Father *changed the channel.*)

MARCOS: Hurry up, *papí.* I want to watch the Charger game.

FATHER: (*Getting excited because the Chivas are about to score.*) *Ya tira. Tira. Tira. Ves, mijo, no saben cerrar. Ya saquen la pelota. Saquenla ya. Pasala burro, pasala. Ya ves, mijo. Es una tontería eso. Asi no se juega el futbol.*

MARCOS: (*Doesn't seem too excited. He's just sitting there watching his* Father.) Ok, ok, let me watch the game.

FATHER: *No, mijo. Este sí es deporte.* American football isn't a sport. You don't need talent to play. *Mira pasala, menso. Aaahhhhgg. Mira, mijo. Mira, mira.* (*Rubs his hands, grabs a rubber chicken from underneath the couch and does a "brujería dance" with the chicken.*)

MARCOS: *Papí,* that doesn't work. Those voodoo *brujería* days are over. Come on, dad. Let me watch the Chargers.

FATHER: (*Not paying any attention to* Marcos.) *Tira ya. Ya suelta la pelota. ¡Ya! Pasala, pasala. Arteaga está abierto ya. Bueno burla, tira ya muchacho. Ya.* Gol!! Goool!!! Goool!! (*Runs around excitedly. He hugs* Marcos, *shaking him.* Marcos *is not happy or excited at all.*) *¡Vieja, las Chivas! ¡Que golaso!* (Mom *walks in and* Marcos *changes the channel.*) Goooll!!! (*Runs to hug* Mom.) *Golaso, vieja.* (*Tries to pick* Mom *up but she takes her* chancla *off and hits him with it.*)

MOM: The last time the *Chivas* beat America I ended up in the hospital because you almost broke my back. *Calmate, viejo.* (*Excited about the game.*) Who scored the goal? Let me see. Marcos, put it back on the soccer game.

MARCOS: *Ayyyy, amá.*

MOM: Now!! (Marcos *changes the channel and she watches the replay for a while.*) Wow!! Who's that young kid? What a great player!

FATHER: His last name is Arteaga. *Le dicen "El Churro".* Great player, *vieja. Mira como se lleva la defensa, y ese tiro.* He plays like I used to play, remember?

MOM: Hhmmmm. No. I don't remember you ever playing soccer like that, *viejo.* Sorry. But that boy sure is good. I haven't seen a player that good in a long time. (*Walks over to the kitchen to prepare lunch for* Father.) *¿Como dijiste que se llama?*

FATHER: Le dicen "*El Churro*".

MARCOS: (*Whining.*) Can I watch the Charger game now?

MOM: *Ay viejo, no te digo.* Listen to this boy. Now he doesn't even like soccer. *Dios mio que barbaridad.*

FATHER: *Ay mijo*, don't you know the importance of this game? Why do you watch the Chargers anyway, *mijo*? Don't they always lose?

MARCOS: (*Bothered.*) Not all the time, *papí*.

FATHER: Oh yeah. My boss says they only lose on Sundays. Is that true, *mijo*? I don't really understand all that stuff.

MARCOS: (*Annoyed.*) *Ya, ya*, ok, ok. I just want to watch the game.

FATHER: *Bueno mijo*, when they finish losing, make sure you mow the lawn and throw out the trash. I need to go to work. Did you hear me, *muchacho*?

MARCOS: (*Not really paying attention.*) Yes, *papí. Sí, sí, sí.* (*Yelling at the television.*) Come on, catch the ball. Damn, the Chargers suck! This is the last game I'm ever watching!

MOM: Where are you going to work today, Jorge?

FATHER: I have the dream job today, *vieja*. I'm going to work on a *nopal* garden. Can you believe that? They want me to take care of the garden every Sunday. Vieja, the dream your mom was talking about is coming true.

MOM: This is a good sign, Jorge. Just be careful, don't start stealing the *nopales* and end up losing your job.

FATHER: No, this gets even better. I can bring home as many *nopales* as I want. Isn't that great, Marcos? Maybe next time you can even help me on the *nopal* garden.

MARCOS: Yeah sure, *papí*. (*Softly.*) Yeah right.

MOM: That's why I married you, *viejo*. I knew someday you would be able to supply me with all the *nopales* I ever wanted. What a dream come true. Oh and Jorge, don't forget your lunch. It's your favorite *tacos de nopales con queso fresco*.

FATHER: (*Walks over to hug and kiss* Mom.) *Gracias, vieja.* You're the best.

MOM: (*Pushes* Father.) *Ya callate* and go to work.

FATHER: Just a little kiss. Come on, *vieja*.

MOM: No! You men are all the same. *Un besito* and then you want to take me to the room for a quick *chaka chaka* or whatever you pigs call it.

FATHER: That's the last thing on my mind. Come on, Dolores, the love of my life. (*Kneels.*)

MOM: Get out of here! Come on. You think I don't know you?

FATHER: *Ay mujer*, after twenty-two years you still don't know me. But if you're interested in a quickie wicky let's go. I have five minutes.

MOM: *Sacate, viejo.* Get out of my house.

FATHER: (*Exits.*) She loves me. She loves me not.

MOM: Marcos, I heard that little comment you made, *mijo*. It hurts me. How can you not get excited about cutting *nopales* with your father? That's every boy's dream in Mexico.

What's wrong with you, Marcos? That's exactly why you're going
to Mexico with us. Last year you started speaking Spanish with a
gringo accent and then you quit watching soccer games with your
father. *Ay, Marcos. ¿Que te pasa?* And how come the other day
I overheard you telling someone that you're Spanish? Marcos, we're
not Spanish! *Somos Mexicanos, Indios.*

MARCOS: But you said we had Spanish blood. I just happen to love my
Spanish blood more. What's wrong with that, mom? And Candy
likes my Spanish blood, too.

MOM: Candy *tus nalgas*. If she loves you, she wouldn't care if you were
Spanish, French or Indochinese.

MARCOS: (*Excited.*) Wow, we have French and Indochinese blood too? I
knew I had French blood! Wait until I tell Candy! And
Indochinese blood too! That sounds so exotic. She's going to love it.

MOM: ¡*Dios mio, Marcos*! ¡*Estás menso*! (*Slaps* Marcos *on the head.*) Now I
understand why your grandma sounds so urgent about getting you
back home to Mexico.

MARCOS: Mommm. (*Whining.*) Ok, let me watch the game. (Mom *walks
away mumbling about her whining* Son. Marcos *screams.*) Throw the
flag! Throw the flag! Uhhh, a blind man could see that's pass
interference.

MOM: (Father *enters.*) *Viejo*, you have to talk to Marcos. Now he thinks
he's French and Indiochinese. I think we need to leave tonight, we
may not get there in time. The boy is losing his identity too fast.

FATHER: Calm down, *vieja*. It'll be fine. ¿*Chino*? Where did that come
from? (Mom *stays staring at him.*) Ok, ok. I'll talk to him. (Marcos
is still yelling at the television.) Marcos, how many times do I have to
tell you? It's just a game of American football. Don't overreact. You
need to control yourself a bit more. I don't know where you get that
from. I didn't raise you to act like that, especially over American
football. (*Exits.*)

MOM: (*Yelling* at Father.) Is that your talk? I never said anything about
a stupid football game. *Ay dios mio*, why did you make men? Why?
(*Day dreaming.*) Imagine a world with just women. (*Snaps out of her
daydream.*) ¡*Los hombres no sirven para nada*! Good for nothing men.
(*Goes to the kitchen.*)

MARCOS: Yes, yeah!!!!! Oh come on Chargers. 4th down. Go for it. Go.
We need a touchdown. Come on, guys. (*Looks around to see if* Mom
*is looking. When he notices that nobody is
watching, he takes the chicken out from
underneath the couch and does the brujería
dance so that his team will score. Afterwards, he sits down calmly and*

nopal boy

looks around just to double-check Mom *didn't see him.*)
   Come on, guys. Let's get the ball in. Handoff. Go to the right, to the right. Yes! Go, go, go! YESSSSS!!!!! Touchdown!!! (*Runs towards* Mom *and is about to hug her, but she waves a big spoon at him. He consciously avoids her and runs around the house.*) Touchdown San Diego! (*Does a little dance in front of the television.*) We scored, mom! We scored!

MOM: We? You didn't do anything, Marcos. You just sat there yelling at that dumb television. I think you need to do what your father said. Now!

MARCOS: I know. I'm going right now.

MOM: Do you remember what your father told you to do?

MARCOS: Yeah.

MOM: *Pues hazlo ahorita.* Knowing you, Marcos, you've already forgotten.

MARCOS: (*Pensive.*) No, I haven't. Uh, what did he tell me?

MOM: *Ay, pinche muchacho. ¡Que saques la basura* and mow the lawn! I'm starting to believe what your father says. You do have brain damage.

MARCOS: Ok, *ya.* Hey mom, I'm hungry. What are we gonna eat?

MOM: *Pues nopales con huevos.* There's nothing like cactus and eggs, *mijo.*

MARCOS: *Nopales?* Cactus? What?! I hate cactus. Mom, we're in America now not the *rancho.*

MOM: (*Shocked.*) ¡¡¿¿Que??!! *Ay muchacho,* in a few days you'll be in Mexico. Yes, Mexico, whether you like it or not. It's for your own good, *muchacho malcriado.* So get used to the *nopales* they may save your life one day.

MARCOS: (*Frustrated.*) Ok, ok. Where did you get those *nopales* from anyway?

MOM: Well you know, *mijo,* your *chango* father cut them over there on the 5 freeway, over where that big Cinderella castle is in La Jolla. But your father said now he'll be able to get nopales straight from his work. Isn't that great? *Ay gracias a la santísima virgin y a todos los santos de mi pueblo.* (*Makes the sign of the cross.*)

MARCOS: Mom! I can't believe what I'm hearing. Cutting *nopales* off freeways? That's illegal! Don't you know? Geez, I can't believe this family. (*Walks out to throw out trash.*)

MOM: I just don't know where we went wrong with that boy. We've given him everything. We work hard to buy him what he wants. *Dios mio.* What went wrong? (*Convincing herself.*) Everything will be ok. Once we go back to Mexico, everything will be just fine.

It won't be too late for my Marquitos. (*Looks at watch.*) Oh the news. Let me get a quick news update. (*Grabs the remote and changes the channel. Video comes on.*)

SCENE TWO: Cactus Gardens Video

AURELIA: Hello this is Aurelia Zuniga from CNN. We're here live in Nopal Heights where several homes have sprouted cactus gardens overnight. Let's see what the residents are saying about this bizarre phenomenon. (*She sees* Chunky. *He's carrying a microwave that he's stealing from a home.*) Hello sir. How are you doing?

CHUNKY: (*Apprehensive.*) I'm fine. Just... uuumm helping my friends move.

AURELIA: What a generous friend. Can you tell us your name?

CHUNKY: Oh yea, Chunky but they call me Chunky.

AURELIA: Wow that's very profound, Mr. Chunky. So where are the rest of your friends?

CHUNKY: They'll be back soon. I probably won't be here when they get back, you know. I have some other errands to run.

AURELIA: Well Mr. Chunky are you one of the residents whose home just sprouted a cactus garden overnight?

CHUNKY: Well yea, Miss News Reporter. A couple of days ago I was helping some other friends down the street move. I started noticing all of these cactus popping out everywhere, you know like popcorn. Pop, pop, pop, just popping up. I saw them popping up in front of my eyes. It was like an acid trip you know, not that I've been on one, but from what I hear, you know. I was a little worried for a while though, I thought maybe it was some kind of surveillance.

AURELIA: Surveillance? I'm a little confused.

CHUNKY: Well you know. I thought maybe the cactus were fake, you know. Maybe someone had cameras hidden inside. You know what I mean? Some high tech Aztec *chingadera* neighborhood watch through cactus. I was tripping Miss News Reporter.

AURELIA: Wow. Well folks, there you have it. A loving caring neighbor who has been a witness to what everyone has been talking about. Pop, pop, pop the cactus came up, he claims. However, we still don't know how all of these cactus gardens popped up over night. Is this a horticulture phenomenon or a brilliant surveillance plan? Did Chunky get his name from Chunky Soup or Chunky Monkey the ice cream? Ladies and gentlemen we will stay on location until we find out what is happening here.
Reporting live from Nopal Heights, this is
Aurelia Zuniga. (*Lights down.*)

nopal boy

39

SCENE THREE

MOM: (*Mom is still on the couch when lights go up. Talking to herself.*)
Right here in our neighborhood? That is the craziest thing I have
ever seen. Now that I think about it, our *nopal* garden has been
growing awfully fast. *Pues más nopales* to eat. I have a lot to clean
around here. (*Turns the radio on and the Selena song "Como la flor"
plays. She sings while mopping the floor.*)

MARCOS: Mom! Mom! (*Walks back in.*) What the …?

MOM: (*Clearing her throat.*) Uuummm, you already cut the grass? That sure
was fast.

MARCOS: (*Hits his forehead.*) Ohhhhhh! I knew I forgot something. I'll do
it later. (*Sits down.*) Mom, can you serve me? Please?

MOM: I thought you didn't like *nopales, gringo.* Plus, *mijito,* do I look like
your maid? *Sirvete, flojo. Yo no soy tu criada.* This is the '90s. *La
mujer* is *libre,* free, free *como los pajaros.* (*She's dressed like a maid
because she's going to work.* Marcos *rolls his eyes and goes over to get his
food.*)

MARCOS: Hey mom, when we go to Mexico, we're not going to eat in
those poor places are we? It's disgusting. Those dogs growling,
looking for food, it grosses me out.

MOM: *¿De que estás hablando? ¿En el mercado?* That's where the best food
is. *Estás loco. Ya te crees muy gringo, tu muchacho.*

MARCOS: No. You know it's kind of gross, mom. (*As they're talking, the
phone rings.*)

MOM: (*Picks up the phone.*) Hello? Who? No, no, I think you got the
wrong number. Nobody by the name of Mark lives here.

MARCOS: It's for me, mom. (*Mom rolls her eyes and gives him the phone.*)
Hello. Oh, hi, Candy. Yea, that was my mom. Where does she
work? Um, she's a, um, a domestic engineer. No, she didn't go to
college for that. She's a very smart woman. Yeah, I just finished
eating. I ate some *nopal,* hamburgers. Yeah, they were good. (*The
moment he says that, he feels a pain on his forehead.*) Ouch! I don't
know I just got a sharp pain on my forehead. Oh yeah, we're still
leaving tomorrow. Yeah, we're going to stay in all the nice hotels
in Mexico, I'm looking forward to doing the tourist thing you know.
(*He feels another pain. He reacts by touching his forehead.*) Oh yea, I
get along with the Mexicans fine. (*Another pain, he drops the phone
and grabs his forehead with both hands.*) Ouch! I'll call you
later bye. (*He hangs up and walks over to a mirror. He sees
a big cactus on his forehead and screams.*) ¡¡Ahhhhhh,
ammáááá!! (Mom *comes running in. Physically there isn't a cactus on his
forehead, but he sees and feels one.*)

Teatro Izcalli

MOM: *¿Mijo, que tienes?*

MARCOS: Look, mom! Look!

MOM: *¿Qué mijo? ¿Qué?*

MARCOS: Can't you see? (*Has a heavy Anglo accent.*) *Tengo un nopal en la frente.* There's a freaking cactus growing on my forehead!

MOM: *Mijo,* I think you're going crazy. Marcos, people can't grow *nopales* out of their foreheads. That's impossible.

MARCOS: Mom, are you even listening to me, can't you see it? It's giving me a big headache. I have a *NOPAL* on my freaking forehead. Look, mom. Look!

MOM: (*Looking closely to see if she sees it.*) I think you're just getting nervous about traveling, *mijo.* The *gringos* call it anxiety. You'll be fine. I'll make you some tea for the headache and you can rest.

MARCOS: Ok. So what kind of tea are you making me, mom?

MOM: (*Walks to the kitchen to make tea.*) *¿Pues qué más, mijo? Te de Nopal.* (*Walks in with tea.*) Marcos, do you remember the legend about the great warrior I told you about a long time ago? I spoke to your grandma last night and she wants me tell you that story again. She said it would help you. I have no idea what she's talking about.

MARCOS: (*Upset.*) I don't want to hear it. How's a stupid story going to help me?

MOM: Ok, Marcos get out of here. You're starting to give me anxiety. *Pinche* anxiety! Just get out of here *muchacho*. (Marcos *exits stage.*) Okay it's just his imagination. I'm not going to worry about it. What if it's really true? How could he possibly be growing a cactus? Those are just stories from the *pueblo.* (*She takes a deep breath to calm herself down then exits stage. Lights go down.*)

SCENE FOUR

(Marcos *is asleep snoring on the couch. Lights go up.*)

DR. DICENADA: Yes, Marcos. How can I help you?

MARCOS: What the hell? Who are you? How did you get here?

DR. DICENADA: My friend, I make house calls. You want to see? (*Yells out.*) House! House! House! (*You hear a drum in the background.*) Get it, Marcos? I called the house. Heeeeee, heee, heee, heeeee. Yes, yes, spit it out. Let me know. Don't be afraid. What are you thinking that's making you **nopal boy** blinking?

MARCOS: Am I dreaming, cause you're really scaring me?

DR. DICENADA: Sure you are. If that's what makes you feel good.

41

(*Dr. Dicenada does a funky dance move and he moves closer to* Marcos.) Marcos, you can ask me anything you want. I have 87.3% of all the answers in the world.

MARCOS: Well, um…I was wondering if… um. . . if a person could grow a *nopal*, I mean a cactus out of his forehead?

DR. DICENADA: Well, yes. Of course, of course. Sit down, *mijo*. Let me tell you the truth. First though, do you know someone who is growing a *nopal*? (*He looks closely at him.*) Oh, ooooohhhh. I understand. (Marcos *covers his forehead.*) Well, well, so it's you. Yes, yes, Marcos. Allow me to begin. Can a boy grow a *nopal* out of his forehead? That is the question. In the forty-eight years I have been studying this synopsis, I've reached a heavily over broad generalization that can someday be proven through empirical evidence to be extremely confusing. I have confined a genetic gene that is found in a very small population of Indigenous people. It has shown us some fascinating data that can lead us to an obvious conclusion. Those who have this *nopal* gene have shown something unbelievable and unique to the human body… (*You hear the voice of* Mom *in the background.*)

MOM: (*Offstage.*) Marcos, you need to go to sleep. It's late now and you've been feeling sick.

MARCOS: (*Looks at his watch, then looks at* Dr. Dicenada *and screams.* Dr Dicenada *exits quickly.*) I'm awake! Mom! Mom!

MOM: (*Walks onstage.*) What, Marcos? What?

MARCOS: A man with long hair, a white coat, an ugly scary man. He was just here in my room!

MOM: Yes, Marcos. I understand *mijo*. I was just in the back with Elvis Presley doing laundry, *mijo*. Oh no, I forgot Elvis didn't like Mexican women, that racist pig.

MARCOS: Come on, mom. How come you don't believe me? I'm your baby, mom.

MOM: *Ay sí, ahora sí eres mi baby, ¿verdad, mijo?* Come, *mijo*. I'll tuck you into bed, just like I used to when you were a little *mocoso*. (*Slaps* Marcos *on the head.*)

MARCOS: But mom, this is real for reals.

MOM: Ok *mijo*. Go get some *pan dulce* and milk. You had a bad dream and you need to get some sugar. It'll help you with the *susto*. (Marcos *exits stage.*)

MOM: (*Calls* Grandma *on the phone.*) *Hola mami*. I wish we wouldn't have told Marcos all of those stories. Yes, the boy is scared. Now he believes he's growing a *nopal* out of his forehead. No *mamá*, it can't be true and now he's talking to some man who appeared in his room. I'm not going to worry about it anymore. We'll be in Mexico soon. Marcos is just having anxiety. Anxiety? It's a word all the *gringos* use when you start worrying too much. *Adios mamá, te quiero mucho.*

DR. DICENADA: (*Reappears onstage after* Mom *and* Marcos *exit.*) Because of the factor I have mentioned, this *nopal* gene reacts causinga chemical imbalance that begins to formulate the first signs of (*A slide of Marcos growing a small green thing on his forehead.*) an eczema or for you who don't have the intellectual capacity to understand what I'm saying, a *pinche* rash grows out of the *vato's* tore up forehead. The last step, of course, occurs when the mitochondria begins to overreact with global testicles, sending an excessive release of hemoglobin which leads to the swelling. The swelling gets so inflamed with molecular gas molecules that it finally causes the global testicles to explode, causing an actual rupture of the crust membrane where we begin to see the cactus-like effects on the forehead. The *nopal* continues to grow like any limb of the human body creating an incredible mitosis, which grows into a Pinocchio-like effect. (*Final slide of* nopal *growing on his forehead.*) That is the *Nopal* Mutation Theory that I have coined as Nopalismosis. Any *pinche* questions? (*Exits. Lights go down.*)

SCENE FIVE

MARCOS: (*Lights go up. It's early morning and a rooster crows.* Marcos *wakes up.*) Why in the hell do those damn neighbors have that stupid rooster?! This isn't Mexico. Ouch! Ouch! (*He goes to the mirror.*) Oh my god!! The *nopal's* getting bigger. ¡¡¡*AMÁÁÁ, AMMMÁÁ, AMMMMÁÁ!!!* (Mom's *not home.*) There has to be something I can do. (*Walks towards the living room and the phone rings.*) Umm, hello? Hello? Oh, hi Candy. Yeah, I'll come over before I leave to Mexico. Well, there's one small problem. Oh never mind. All right. See you later. Bye. (Marcos *reaches underneath the couch and pulls out a steering wheel. The sound of a car starting up is in the background as he turns the key. The song "Paradise City" by Guns N Roses plays from his car stereo. He drives for a while.* Marcos *is singing when all of a sudden, a siren comes on behind him.* Cop *rolls out from behind the siren/red light.*)

COP: (*Wearing a demon mask as he rolls onto the stage with gun pointing at* Marcos. *He takes mask off quickly.*) All right, Marcos. Come out with your hands up. (*Walks over to the car,* Marcos *is still in the car, scared to death.* Cop *looks at* Marcos.) I said come out with your hands up,

nopal boy

43

Marcos. And take four steps. (Marcos *steps out of car and does what* Cop *says to do.*) Ok, stop. Simon says, put your right hand over your nose. Simon says put your left hand on your nose. Put your hands over your head. (Marcos *puts his hands up and he loses.* Cop *breaks out laughing.*)

MARCOS: How do you know my name, officer?

COP: I saw it on your driver's license, boy.

MARCOS: But, you haven't even asked me for my drivers license.

COP: (*Raising his voice.*) Who's going to ask the questions around here, me or you?

MARCOS: What's the problem, sir?

COP: Put your hands up against the car. Got any sharp objects, boy? (*Takes out rubber gloves and puts them on.*)

MARCOS: What are you going to do with those?????

COP: I need to search you, boy. You understand. Do me some searching, boy. All right bend over.

MARCOS: (*Looking very scared towards the audience.*) Search??? Where???

COP: Don't worry about it, boy. You just bend over the car. (*Starts to search* Marcos.)

MARCOS: Why are you doing this to me? You must be confusing me for somebody else. (Cop *searches* Marcos *near his legs.*)

MARCOS: ¡Ayy, buey!

COP: Shut up, boy. I just got news that a cactus store was robbed about five minutes ago. The suspect was Mexican, driving a car, and wearing clothes. (*Gets in his face.*) Sounds a lot like you, doesn't it?

MARCOS: (*Holding up his hands over his head so the* Cop *doesn't see the imaginary cactus.*) No, officer. You're definitely confusing me for somebody else. I'm... I'm Spanish, not Mexican. Look, I'm on my way to see my girlfriend. She lives right around the corner.

COP: (*Not really paying attention to* Marcos.) Spanish? Yeah right. Spaniards talk funny. This is La Jolla, you know. I don't think your girlfriend lives around here, buddy. Move! Let me check your car. (*Goes into the car and finds the rubber chicken.*) Aha, so you've been choking the chicken, huh, Marcos?

MARCOS: No officer. My father chokes the chicken when he watches soccer games. It wasn't me. I never choke the chicken.

COP: (*Looks in the car and he can't find anything. Then he pulls a cactus off the side of the stage and throws it in the car.*) Aha! (*Holds up the cactus.*) Do you know what this is boy? Huh? (*Drops nopal on the ground.*) Look at it! Do you know what that is?

MARCOS: (*At the point of crying.*) Yes. Yes.

COP: What is it, boy? What is it? (Cop's *tail comes out and he's trying to hide it.*)

MARCOS: *Es un nopal.* A cactus.

COP: What the hell did you say? English only, Spanish boy! English only! 227 passed. Where have you been? (*Laughs.*) Haaaa haaaa haaa. I could arrest you for talking like that. (*Laughs diabolically.*) Ahaaa haa haaa haaa.

MARCOS: (*Starts to cry.*) It's a cactus. It's a freaking cactus!

COP: You're right, boy. It's a cactus. (*Starts dancing around holding his tail.*) It's a cactus. It's a cactus! Aaah haaa haa haa haa!!! (*He laughs at* Marcos *and lightning goes off in the background. He stops laughing all of a sudden.* Marcos *has fallen to his knees and is quietly whimpering.*) Get up! Let me see your eyes (*Checks his eyes.*)·

MARCOS: I've never been in trouble with the law, never, ever, sir. I don't know where that cactus came from.

COP: (*Slaps Marcos in the butt.*) Ahaa haaa haaa! Have you, or anyone you know, ever picked cactus illegally off the freeway, side roads, in the back of someone's house, etc., etc.?

MARCOS: No, sir. My father has never, ever picked *nopales* illegally off the freeways, side roads, or the back of someone's house, etc., etc., sir.

COP: What did you just say about your father? Your father picks cactus off the freeways? (*Pulls his gun half way out then puts it back in its holster because he sees someone coming. He then vanishes.*)

MARCOS: What? (*Confused.*) Candy? (Anglo Woman *enters.*)

ANGLO WOMAN: Hi. I was wondering if you would sign this petition to keep illegal aliens out of our land. Aliens are responsible for the destruction of our cactus plants. (*Whispers.*) They eat them you know. You know, our economy depends heavily on the cactus plant. Did you know that Mexican aliens stole and ate more than twenty tons of cactus in the last two years? It almost destroyed California's economy! (Marcos *is hiding his head so that she won't see his cactus.* Anglo Woman *screams.*) Oh, my god! You're one of them! You're one of them! Aaahh! Aahhh! It's an alien! An alien! (*Exits screaming.*)

MARCOS: How can she think I'm one of them? My god, she must have seen the cactus growing out of my forehead! (*He touches his forehead.*) OUCH!! Where in the world is Candy? What's going on here? Candy! Candyyyyy! (Candy *enters stage. He runs and hugs her.*) You're not going to believe what just happened to me. First a cop harasses me and the. . . (Candy *interrupts him.*)

CANDY: It's ok, Marcos. It's ok. Slow down. You know I'm here for you, my little Spanish *conquistador*.

MARCOS: Oh Candy, when you call me those names, it **nopal boy** makes me forget about the whole world and all of my problems.

45

CANDY: Yes, my little flamingo dancer. (Marcos *stands like a flamingo on one foot.*)

MARCOS: *Olé.*

CANDY: My little cha-cha dancer.

MARCOS: Tell me more. (*Feels a sharp pain on his head.*) Ouchh!!!

CANDY: Marcos, are you ok?

MARCOS: Yeah. I just have a little headache.

CANDY: It's okay Marcos. You're here with me now.

MARCOS: Oh, Candy, you're magical. By the way I found out some new things about my family tree. It turns out that I'm also part French. *Oui, oui.*

CANDY: Wow. How romantic.

MARCOS: No, it gets better. I'm also part Indochinese.

CANDY: (*Puts her arm around him and touches his stomach.*) I knew there was something exotic about you. (Marcos *looks at the audience and winks.*) I'm so glad to hear that Marcos. My father, well, you know how my father feels about me dating you. He keeps saying you're a Mexican. He says "Mexicans are made to work for you. Not to marry." He'll be so happy to hear you're French. And the Indiochinese blood, we'll just keep it to our selves, my sexy karate man. (Marcos *does a karate chop and grunts.*)

CANDY: Marcos, you're getting so strong. Have you been working out? (*He's about to speak and she shushes him.*) Sshhh. It's my father. He's coming around the corner. Just to be safe I think you should leave until I assure him that you're not a Mexican.

MARCOS: I've had too many problems today so I'm out of here. (*He gets in his car.* Candy *exits.*)

DR. DICENADA: (*When the car starts,* Dr. Dicenada *runs on the side and jumps in.*) Well, Marcos, nopalismosis is a dangerous painful process. Yes, it is my friend. But what you must be thinking now is once a person has contracted nopalismosis and the mitochondria has accelerated to its full capacity, what happens? That is exactly what happens Marcos. The mitochondria functions at a superhuman velocity, the individual develops exactly that, a super imposed mitochondria. I have reached the conclusion to your long asked question. The root of the problem may be the root of the solution. Again Marcos listen carefully, the root of the problem is the root of the solution. *Ayyy*, I'm sorry, Marcos. *Adios.* (*He falls on the ground and rolls off stage. Lights go down. Lights come back on slowly.* Marcos *is center stage, out of the car. He's kneeling, going into his Shakespearean moment.**)

MARCOS: Fie. Why hast thou forsaken me, oh *nopal?* Thine prickly needles rest on my head. Dost though have no mercy? Taketh yourself from

my *pinche* head. My own hands art full of your stench. Refuse thou *futbol* and deny my identity. For a *nopal* by any other name still hurts. . . when I touch it. (*Touches forehead*). Ouch!
(*Transition: Slides of* Father *cutting* nopales *on the freeway.*)

Shakespearean moment written by Cristina Nuñez.

SCENE SIX

(Mom, Father and Marcos are *sitting on the couch. The couch has now become an airplane seat.*)

FLIGHT ATTENDANT'S VOICE: (*A* Flight Attendant *enters and acts out what the voice is saying. She's carrying a doll with her.*) *Buenas noches. Bienvenidos a Nopal Alas.* Good evening and welcome to Cactus Airlines, where every plane ride is as smooth as a cactus needle. (Flight Attendant *is holding up a cactus.*) Ladies and gentlemen, the exit signs are to your left. I think, yeah, yeah, to your left. Ladies and gentlemen, the exit signs are broken, and we haven't had time to repair them so, in case of an emergency, please remain seated until we have figured out what the heck to do. If, by any chance, we're going to crash and if you think you're going to die, please take the *nopal* from underneath your seats and begin to eat as much as possible. Always remember, please feed yourself the *nopal* first and then your child. (*She feeds the doll.*) Thank you. Please put your safety belts on and have a smooth flight. (*Sound of airplane taking off is heard.* Marcos, Mom, *and* Father *act as though plane is taking off.*)

MARCOS: Mom, did you hear that? They said that we're going to die.

MOM: Marcos, what are you talking about? They always say that just to make us feel better. Relax, *mijo*. Relax.

MARCOS: Hey mom, do you think anybody has noticed that there's a cactus growing out of my forehead?

MOM: *Mijo*, you're crazy. How many times do I have to tell you that there's no cactus on your forehead!

FATHER: *Mijo, estás menso.* People can't grow a cactus on their forehead, those are old stories from the *pueblo mijo.*

MARCOS: (*Touches his forehead.*) Ouch!!!! Ouch!!!!!

FATHER: *Estás bien menso, mijo.*

FLIGHT ATTENDANT: (*Not friendly.*) Hi. Would you **nopal boy** like something to eat or drink? And hurry up, before I accidentally drop this metal tray on your head.

FATHER: What do you have to eat?

FLIGHT ATTENDANT: We have some *quesadillas de nopales* and peanuts.

FATHER: *Quesadillas de nopales. Sí, sí.* I love those things. Could I also have a cold *nopal* juice please?

MOM: *Viejo pansón.* Don't try to flirt. You think that pretty young lady is ever going to show interest in your big *pansa*?

FATHER: *Vieja,* what are you talking about?

MOM: I saw the way you looked at her, like if she was the last *nopal* left in the desert. Let Marcos order and clean that *baba* off your face.

FATHER: *Aaahhh.*

MOM: *Tu también menso.* (*Hits* Marcos *on the head.*) Order something.

MARCOS: Do you have anything else besides *quesadillas de nopales*?

FLIGHT ATTENDANT: Oh yes, we have pork chops with barbecue beans or perhaps you would be happy with me slapping that cactus off your forehead?

MARCOS: What? Mom, did you hear that?

MOM: Marcos, she's being sarcastic. That's what you get for insulting her like that. (*Mimicking* Marcos.) Do you have anything else? Oh yes, *muy fregon.* Can't eat cactus *quesadillas.* Don't ever insult her like that. Now you apologize for those *tonterías.*

MARCOS: Sorry. (*Talking* to Flight Attendant.)

MOM: He doesn't want anything. Get me a *nopal* on the rocks please. Thank you.

FLIGHT ATTENDANT: You're very welcome. No problem.

MOM: Stop staring. You're embarrassing yourself.

FATHER: I'm not staring. Hey *vieja,* I've always had a fantasy. You know. You and me in an airplane bathroom at fifteen million feet. You know, *chaka chaka.*

MOM: ¡*Cochino!* You know what, Jorge, I'm convinced that they invented Viagra using your hormones. *Cochino.*

FATHER: Come on, Dolores. (*Winks at* Mom *and laughs.*)

MOM: I'm going to tell the whole pueblo that you're a dirty old man. *Vas a ver.*

FATHER: (*Laughs.*) I like you, *vieja,* something about you being feisty.

PILOT'S VOICE: (*Voice is not very clear.*) Good evening, ladies and gentlemen. *Buenas noches, damas y caballeros.* We're approximately twenty-five million feet in elevation. We'll be landing in Guadalajara, Mexico in approximately fifteen minutes. Please stay seated and... (Pilots' *voice gets interrupted by the voice of the* Devil.)

Teatro Izcalli

DEVIL: . . . and you, the boy growing a cactus out of his forehead, no more peanuts for you. Aaa haaa haaa haaa!!!!!

MARCOS: (*Screaming.*) ¡¡*AMMÁÁÁÁ*!! Did you hear that?! They're talking about me. I told you! Everyone knows. They can see it!

48

FATHER: I think someone's doing *brujería* on this boy, Dolores.

MOM: *Viejo*, he's just so scared. I don't think it's anxiety anymore. (*Lights go off and they've arrived at the airport in Mexico.* Marcos, Mom *and* Father *are waiting for their luggage.*)

MARCOS: When is the luggage going to get here? I'm tired of waiting.

MOM: *Mijo*, be patient. You want everything so fast and easy like the *gringo*. You want to microwave life, don't you?

FATHER: *Mijo*, this is Mexico. Everything here goes slow. And the people, we like it that way. There's no hurry. In a hurry is the *diablo*. You know *mijo*, they say the devil himself has no patience. If you really want things in a hurry, the devil, he will give it to you. But you get things so fast you don't know what to do with them and then you end up hurting yourself.

MOM: Yes, *mijo*. The devil appears all over Mexico, all the time.

MARCOS: How come the devil never goes to the United States? I never hear stories of the devil over there.

MOM: *Valgame dios, hijo*. It's not good to make fun of the devil. The devil, he's always around. Remember all the stories your *abuelita* has told you, *mijo*. They're true. And for those that want the fast American dream, *por esos va primero*.

MARCOS: Hey ma, do you think the devil can get rid of this *nopal* on my forehead?

FATHER: *Ay muchacho! No hables asi. El diablo se te va aparecer.* The devil will come out if you talk that way.

MOM: Plus, how many times do we have to tell you? You don't have a *nopal* growing on your forehead! *Pobre mijo*. You watch too much American television. The only good thing about American television *mijo* is "Days of Our Lives." Now that's good television.

FATHER: *Ay vieja, tu también estás loca*.

MARCOS: Mom, how long is the drive from here to *Nopalitlán*?

FATHER: About six hours. We'll go on the bus. We should be there in six hours.

MARCOS: I don't want to go in one of those dumb buses with all those people, chickens, and pigs. Can I just go in a taxi?

MOM: You really do have mental problems, *mijo*. (*Gets mad.*) Look Marcos, if you want to go in a taxi and waste your money, then go ahead.

MARCOS: (*Thinking about it.*) Yeah, I do. I'll go in a taxi on my own.

FATHER: *No estes fregando*. It's better anyways, me and your mom can have a romantic trip on the bus.

MOM: Shut up, *pansón feo*! I changed my mind. He **nopal boy** needs to stay with us. I'm just too worried about him.

FATHER: You're really going crazy *también*.

MOM: (*Hits* Father *with her purse.*) *Viejo pansón.* Carry my luggage. Come on be good for something. All right *mijo* your dad is right, I'm overreacting. Go ahead and go on your own. The taxi will take you straight there. (Marcos *hugs his parents and says goodbye.*)

MARCOS: All right I need some time alone, just to relax, not to think of anything. I need to clear my mind. Bye, mom. Bye, dad. See you at *abuelita's* house.

MOM: *Adios, hijo, y que dios esté contigo.* (*Turns to* Father *sadly.*) Should we let our baby go alone? *Es un pendejo.*

FATHER: He'll be fine Dolores. *Ya está viejo el muchacho. Ya vete, muchacho.* Get out of here. (*Lights start to fade out.* Mom and Father *exit. Lights come back on and* Marcos *is standing center stage with his suitcase.*)

MARCOS: Taxi! Hey taxi!! Hey, why don't any of these taxis stop for me? I know. (*Sits on suitcase.*) It's because I'm Spanish!! (*Suitcase falls and so does* Marcos.) Agghh! (*Lights down.*)

SCENE SEVEN: Marcos Neighbors' Video

(Aurelia Zuniga *reporting live from Nopal Heights with local residents.*)

AURELIA: We're here live in Nopal Heights at the home of the Sanchez family. As some of you may recall, last week cactus started growing abundantly in the neighborhood. As you can see, the cactus have completely taken over the home of the Sanchez family. Residents say that as soon as the Sanchez family left to Mexico, these giant cactus grew over night, making it impossible for anyone to even reach the front door. What's more strange is what neighbors are sharing about a boy named Marcos, who lives here. To my left is one of the neighbors. Dude, could you tell us about your interaction with Marcos?

DUDE: Yea first can I ask my mom something? (*Pulls up his shirt and points at his nipple.*) Hey mom, can I get... like a nipple ring? (*Puts his shirt down.*) Oh. Well one time when Marcos and I went to Roberto's I noticed he was growing a (*Grabs a cactus from the nopal garden.*) killer cactus from his forehead.

AURELIA: Yes. And then what happened?

DUDE: I asked him, hey dude can you like make a *quesadilla* with that?

AURELIA: And then what was the dramatic outcome?

Teatro Izcalli DUDE: He called me a *pendejo.* It was so gnarly, tubular cool.

AURELIA: He called you a *pendejo.* You heard it live. By the way nice tan, Dude. (Dude *exits.*) And here to my right are two women who claim

50

they have spent time with the boy and his family.

COMADRE 1: Yes, I've known the boy since he was a baby. I used to babysit him and have to change his *cacarocha*. (*Turns to her* comadre.) *Comadre* remember he had some strong *cacarocha*. *Sí, muy fuerte.* One time I remember seeing cactus needles in his *cacarocha*. Yes. I read in *Alarma* Magazine that cactus needles in *cacarocha* was a sign. I think Marquito's special, but nobody believes me, just because they say I'm the *chismosa* of the *barrio*. (*Walks away, calling out to her friend.*) ¡Doña Paquita! ¡Doña Paquita! ¿Dejeme contarle algo?

AURELIA: Incredible accounts. This woman says she noticed cactus needles in what she refers to as his *cacarocha*. She also claims that this is a sign. (*Approaches* Comadre 2.) And you mam?

COMADRE 2: *Ay dios mio.* I've known the family for many years and I always knew there was something *especial* about Marquitos. Oh yes, not only did I see the *nopal* on his forehead but I also saw the apparition of the Virgen of Guadalupe. Yes I did. *Santa Maria, madre de dios ruega …* (*Walks off praying.*)

AURELIA: Simply incredible. As of right now we're not sure where the family is. What are the signs telling us? Does the family have cactus home insurance? Will Dude's mom let him get a nipple ring? Reporting live from *Nopal* Heights, this is Aurelia Zuniga for CNN. (*End of video. Lights go up.*)

SCENE EIGHT

(Marcos and Taxi Driver a*re sitting on couch, which is now a taxi. The* Taxi Driver *is driving. Scene starts with both of the characters singing* "Calaveras y Diablitos" *by the* Fabulosos Cadillacs.)

TAXI DRIVER: So where are you going, my friend?

MARCOS: I'm going to *Nopalitlán*. Can you take me there?

TAXI DRIVER: I sure can, my friend Marcos. Anything you want.

MARCOS: How did you know my name?

TAXI DRIVER: Well, you won't believe it, Marcos. But last night I had a dream, my friend. Yeah. In that dream, I dreamt about a boy just like you and he wanted to go to *Nopalitlán*. I remember him telling me that his name was Marcos.

MARCOS: Wow, that's pretty cool.

TAXI DRIVER: So Marcos, you're from San Diego?

MARCOS: How did you know that?

TAXI DRIVER: Uumm, I saw the tags on your luggage. That's how I know. I used to have a friend in that area. He was a police officer. I haven't

nopal boy

51

seen him in a couple of years. So Marcos, you like living in the United States?

MARCOS: Yes and I'm proud to be an American.

TAXI DRIVER: (*Starts singing.*) And I'm proud to be an American because at least I know I'm free. Ha ha ha ha ha! Wow. Wouldn't you like to be a rich and famous American someday? Perhaps a soccer star like that young man, Arteaga. You know who he is, right?

MARCOS: Yea, my dad thinks that he sold his soul to the devil, because all of a sudden he plays like the best in the world.

TAXI DRIVER: (*Laughs.*) Ha ha ha ha ha!! Your dad is very crazy, my friend. The devil isn't always so bad, he gives you a lot of power you know. If you work carefully with him, he can give you a lot more than you think. You know, like in the movies.

MARCOS: But that's just in the movies. Well, all this talking is making me hungry. Is there a Jack in the Box around here? I could go for a bacon cheeseburger and some french fries. (*To himself.*) What a dumb question. There's no Jack in the Box around here.

TAXI DRIVER: You know what, Marcos? (*Jumps over the couch and starts pulling out all kinds of objects.*) You are lucky, my friend. (*Pulls out a Jack in the Box bag with a bacon cheeseburger, french fries, and a coke.*) I always have an extra Jack in the Box with me.

MARCOS: Wow! That was something. (*Looks in the bag.*) How did you do that? And it's still warm. (*Amazed. Takes a bite out of the cheeseburger.*)

TAXI DRIVER: Let's just say that Jack and I, *pues, somos amigos.* I know Jack very well. I've helped him get to where he is today. (*Laughing hysterically.*) Ahh ha ha ha ha ha!!!

MARCOS: You really know Jack?

TAXI DRIVER: Long story my friend.

MARCOS: You know I had a real hard time getting a taxi. Nobody would stop for me. It was like I didn't exist. All of the sudden you showed up out of nowhere. Like an angel to the rescue.

TAXI DRIVER: (*Screams.*) Agggghhhhh!!! (*Stands up.*) ¡Pinche vaca! (*Sound of a cow mooing.*) I'll see you at the next *carne asada.*

TAXI DRIVER: Yes, Marcos. To the rescue I have come, to save you from a lot of misery and pain. Well, we're almost in *Nopalitlán,* about another hour or so.

MARCOS: (*Spits out some of his food.*) One more hour? That's impossible! My mom said it took six hours to get there. I don't believe this. I don't even think we're going the right way. That sign said Nopalitlán was the other way. (*Thinking.*) You have a very familiar laugh you know.

TAXI DRIVER: You know *amigo,* I found the ultimate way of cheating life.

Teatro Izcalli

52

Yeah. Sure did. Stay young forever.

MARCOS: How?

TAXI DRIVER: Guess.

MARCOS: I have no idea.

TAXI DRIVER: You have no idea, do you? I work for someone who has a lot of power. Listen, Marcos, I have a piece of paper in that bag. Why don't you pull it out and read it? (Marcos *pulls out a long piece of paper.*) You know, I could make all of your dreams come true, even make your skin color change. Doesn't that sound great? I could make you live the American Dream... money...fame. Anything you want, my friend. Just sign here. Better yet Marcos, you and I could rule the world together.

MARCOS: Rule the world together? You're funny. I'd just like to be a football star.

TAXI DRIVER: A football star? Think bigger, boy. Bigger. (*Yells.*) Just sign, *muchacho*!

MARCOS: I'm not really sure. Let me just read a bit more. What does acclimate mean?

TAXI DRIVE: (*Raising his voice.*) Marcos, we're running out of time! You need to sign or else... (*Pulls out a knife and all of a sudden he slams the breaks, screaming.*) ¡¡Pinches nopales!! (*Sound of car crashing. Lightning in the background.*)

MARCOS: ¡¡¡¡Ammáááááá!!!!

(*Lights down and* La Banda del Carro Rojo *song comes on.*)

SCENE NINE

(Marcos is *lying in bed, slowly waking up.* Mom *and* Grandma *are standing by the bed.*)

MARCOS: Mamí, mamí . . . (*Waking up from a nightmare.*)

FATHER: ¡¿Y yo que muchacho?!

MARCOS: Where am I?

GRANDMA: Aquí, hijo. En mi casa.

MARCOS: (*Recognizing his* Grandma's voice. He's happy.) Abuelita, abuelita.

MOM: Mamí, we'll be right back. I'm going to get the herbs that you need. (Mom *and* Father *exit.*)

GRANDMA: Sí, hija. (*She reaches down to hug* Marcos.) Mijo, you'll be fine.

MARCOS: (*Sniffing clothes.*) Abuelita, what's that smell?

GRANDMA: Pues vaporu, hijito. (*Takes vaporub out of blouse.*) It cures everything. (*Places vaporub on the table and walks back to* Marcos.)

MARCOS: ¿Abuelita, que me pasó?

nopal boy

53

GRANDMA: You were in an accident *mijo*. *El* taxi crashed when it slipped on a cactus on the road.

MARCOS: (*Alarmed and scared.*) The taxi driver!!!! *Era el diablo, abuelita. ¡¡¡¡¡Era el diablo!!!!!*

GRANDMA: *No, Marquitos.* The *diablo* no show around here no more.

MARCOS: (*Speaking fast.*) *No abuelita.* It was the devil. He brought me a bacon cheeseburger and he told me we would get to your house in an hour.

GRANDMA: *Valgame dios, Marquitos. ¿Que es un* bacon cheeseburger?

MARCOS: *Nada, abuelita.*

GRANDMA: *No, mijo.* They found you in a cactus garden. *Sí, en un jardin de nopales.*

MARCOS: *Abuelita,* I flew through the window? I have no broken bones? In the cactus garden I felt so... I can't explain. I felt at home like someone was protecting me.

GRANDMA: Yes *mijo*, that's a good thing.

MARCOS: What? (*Confused.*)

GRANDMA: We have a lot of time to talk *mijo*. I'll explain it all to you. (*Walks over and grabs some tea.*) *Ten mijo, tomate este té y luego a dormir.*

MARCOS: (*Takes a sip and makes an ugly face.*) Eeeuuu.

GRANDMA: *Pero tomatelo todo.* Drink it all. (*Holds cup until he drinks it all.*)

MARCOS: *Gracias, abuelita.* (*Gets comfortable to go back to sleep.*)

GRANDMA: *De nada, hijito. Ay,* Marcos. *No has venido en cinco años, pero yo te he visto todos los días,* your pain living in the other side. I see that pain in so many over there. I was worried you would not make it here. We're very lucky he did not get to you. *Descansa, mijo. Descansa.*

MARCOS: (*Half-asleep.*) *¿Que?* I don't understand, *abuelita.*

GRANDMA: *Está bien, mijo.* Get some rest. (*Walks over to table and lights a candle and* copal *in a* sahumero. *Then walks over to* Marcos *and does a* limpia. *Indigenous music plays.*)

DEVIL: (*Underneath the bed and then suddenly pops out.*) And now young Marcos, you shall die.

GRANDMA: *¡Detente, Satanaz!* (*Raises her hand and the* Devil *falls.*)

DEVIL: Uh huh, so we finally meet old lady. And I see you have some powers of your own.

GRANDMA: You thought you had won when you killed my great, great, grandfather.

DEVIL: I have taken many more since that day. (*Pulls out a gun from the Mexican Revolution.*)

GRANDMA: Did that belong to Zapata? (Devil *nods his head.*) You killed

54

Zapata? He was our last hope.

DEVIL: And who can forget this one. (*Takes out a mask of El Santo Enmascarado de Plata.*)

GRANDMA: And you had to kill *El Santo* too? ¡*Desgraciado*!

DEVIL: Yes and when I finish with you, the boy will be next. He'll never reach his full potential.

GRANDMA: (*Yelling.*) Noo!! This one's for the people of the sun! (*Boxing bell rings and "People of the Sun" song by Rage Against the Machine plays, as they fight. Finally the Grandma is about to get killed as she falls to the ground. The Devil pulls out a big knife.*)

DEVIL: (*About to kill Grandma.*) And now old lady you can go and meet your ancestors.

MARCOS: (*Jumps up from the bed.*) No! (*Raises his hand and the Devil falls down from the force. The knife falls towards Marcos and he picks it up.*)

DEVIL: You foolish boy, don't do it. We could both rule the world together. Do you not see it? I'll teach you how to use your powers.

MARCOS: What are you talking about?

DEVIL: The times have changed boy, we can be united.

GRANDMA: Don't listen *mijo*. Don't listen to him.

MARCOS: (*Charges after Devil with the knife. He's about to kill him when Devil throws a spark on stage and disappears.*)

DEVIL: I'll be back. (*Laughs.*) Aaaah haaaa haaa.

GRANDMA: Mijo. (*Runs and hugs him.*) You did it, *mijo*. You were able to use your powers.

MARCOS: It's all starting to make sense. *Abuelita*, the story of the warrior and the cactus. I saw it all when I was lying in the cactus garden.

GRANDMA: *Sí, hijo.* It all started five hundred years ago when the Spanish landed on this continent. They captured one of our warriors. They beat him and left him to die in a desert full of cactus. Little did they know that the warrior knew how to survive by just eating the cactus. Years went by and that was all this warrior ate. He hid out there because he knew what was happening to his people. When he finally returned years later he saw that thousands had died because of disease, slavery, and murder. This warrior though became so strong from the cactus that he gained super powers. He helped lead a resistance against the Spanish and eventually moved thousands of our people back to this mountain where our *cultura* has survived for hundreds of years. He went on to help many other tribes on this continent from becoming extinct. He lived to be 260 years old, but even his powers could **nopal boy** not stop death. We knew one day his super-powers would show up in one of his great great grandchildren. That child would grow up to fight for justice for all people.

55

MARCOS: And who is that *abuelita*? Is he here in Mexico? Can we meet him?

GRANDMA: It's you, *baboso*! Holy *frijoles*.

MARCOS: Oh yea. I get it.

GRANDMA: (*She pulls out a superhero costume with a nopal on the shirt.*) One day you'll fulfill your destiny. (*Lights fade out quickly and come back on.* Grandma *has exited stage.*)

MARCOS: (*On the phone, speaking loudly.*) Hello Candy. I'm doing great. Better than I thought. Hey Candy, I have to tell you something. I'm Mexican ... (*Lights go down.*)

SCENE TEN: At the Border Video

AURELIA: To all of you viewers who have been following the cactus mystery, we feel that we may be unraveling the truth. Residents from Nopal Heights have been talking about an old Mexican Indigenous legend. The cactus have made a trail from Nopal Heights to this very location, the border town of San Ysidro. Residents say that at the end of the trail an old legend will come to life. But what is that old legend? And will it really come to life here, at the heart of controversy where the minutemen have been clashing with activists? Yes, we have been getting reports from community activists that people calling themselves minutemen have been patrolling the border and physically hurting innocent women and children crossing the border. Wait, wait, I hear screams. Oh my god, what is going on? (*A man appears next to* Aurelia. *He has a* nopal *stuck in his neck and he's in pain.*) Sir, what happened?

MINUTE MAN: We're being attacked by cactus from the sky. (*Points up to the sky.*)

AURELIA: Ladies and gentlemen, this is the most remarkable thing I have ever seen. A man is actually flying and cactus are flying from out of his forehead. And with perfect aim, he's hitting the minutemen. The minutemen are running back to their cars, screaming in pain. This is unbelievable! There are so many more questions unanswered. Who is this mysterious man? And how did he find a way to fly? Who will be the next victim of his cactus throwing abilities? Will I marry a Mexican and enjoy watching *telenovelas*? Reporting live from the San Ysidro border, this is Aurelia Zuniga. (*Start's running and ducking.*) This is crazy!

Teatro Izcalli

(*End of play.*)

56

Cast members during 1997.
(Back left.) Victor Chavez Jr., Maria Figueroa, Alicia Chavez,
Macedonio Arteaga Jr., Miguel-Angel Soria.
(Front left.) Benny Madera and Iyari Arteaga.
Photo by Angel Nevarez.

Got Tortillas? 1997.
Artwork by Posada.
Flyer design by Larry Baza.

nopal boy

entro Cultural de la Raza *presents*

Teatro Izcalli Sin Verguenza

November 20-21 at 7pm
Sunday 22nd at 2pm

Adults $10
Students $8

2004 Park Blvd
Balboa Park

call 235-6135
for reservations

a Xaxro production

performing **"El Nopal Boy"** *an original comedy*

Nopal Boy, 1998. (Top left to right.) Alicia Chavez, Cristina Nuñez, Victor Chavez Jr., Michelle Tellez, Macedonio Arteaga Jr., Ricky Medina. (Front left to right.) Benny Madera, Abel Macias, Iyari Arteaga, Claudia Cuevas. Photo by Pablo Hernandez. Flyer design by Gabriel Benitez.

Cast and crew of Nopal Boy, 1998.
At the Centro Cultural de la Raza in San Diego.

Teatro Izcalli

Nopal Boy, 1998.
(Left to right.) Claudia Cuevas, Alicia Chavez, Victor Chavez Jr.
Photo by Jose Luis Lepe.

Nopal Boy cast members, 1999.
Left: Victor Chavez Jr., Benny Madera, Ricky Medina,
Hector Villegas, Macedonio Arteaga, Jr.
Photo by Alicia Chavez.

nopal boy

Teatro Izcalli

Parody a lo Chicano

Bosque Gump is one of the original sketches written by our group. It was initially written by Alicia Chavez and myself. It was then taken back to the group where we received additional input mainly from Benny Madera who has been the only person who has ever played this character. This *acto* was created when Forrest Gump was at the movies. It was such a popular movie but once again it failed to show any representation of Chicanos/Latinos in Vietnam or in the civil rights movement.

BOSQUE GUMP
By Teatro Izcalli

CHARACTERS:

OLD LADY - An older lady in her sixties, wearing glasses, with grey hair, dressed in a long skirt, and carrying a purse.
BOSQUE GUMP - A Chicano version of Forrest Gump. Character should be dressed like Forrest and with a southern accent.
LITTLE GIRL - Around nine years and holding a lollipop.
TWO HIPPIES - Wearing old jeans and tie-dye shirts, with long hair or an afro.

Props: A bench, some feathers, a suitcase for Bosque Gump, a low-rider bike, low-rider bike magazines, and a giant *saladito*.

(Scene begins with Forrest Gump theme song. Bosque *walks up to the bench.* Old Lady *and* Little Girl *are already sitting there. A chicken clucks in the as background someone runs across the stage throwing feathers in the air.)*

BOSQUE: Hello. My name is Bosque, Bosque Gump. But my real name is
   Bosque Eduardo Conchita Alonzo Ochoa Barbacoa Chávez Martínez
   Castillo Platillo Tutillo Valladolid Guevarra Gump. (Old Lady *looks
   a bit annoyed* and moves over.) Would you like a *saladito*? (*Pulls out a
   giant* saladito, *the size of a soccer ball.*)
OLD LADY: *No. No gracias.*
BOSQUE: My momma always said life was like a bag of *saladitos.* You never
   know how sour it's going to be until you suck on it.
OLD LADY: ¡*Viejo, asqueroso!* (Old Lady *gets up and does a karate kick and
   and he falls to the ground.*)
LITTLE GIRL: (*Mocking* Bosque.) Chusma, chusma, brrr. (Bosque *gets up
   and has a huge swollen eye. He licks his giant saladito and makes
   a sour face.*)
BOSQUE: You know, that reminds me of the day my second grade teacher,
   Ms. Cornelia, hit me for speaking Spanish. She was a brown woman
   of Mexican descent. I think she was ashamed of her culture so much
   that she hated herself and anyone like her. She said if I wanted to
   speak Spanish my little bandit butt should go back to Mexico.
   That's all I have to say about that. (*He pauses for a few seconds.*) You
   know, I don't know why I'm talking like this if I'm Chicano.
   Because I talk like this, some people think I'm from Kentucky.
   Those people call me KFC- Kentucky Fried Chicano. You know, I
   don't know why there weren't any more Chicanos in the Vietnam
   part of my movie. After all, 83,000 *raza* served in Vietnam. Of those
   83,000 *raza,* 20% were killed, and 33% were injured. That's all I
   have to say about that. I remember the first time I was coming back
   from Tijuana. I was going to visit my momma. Some men in green
   uniforms stopped me. They said I couldn't come over because I wasn't
   American. There was no way those green men were going to stop me
   from seeing my momma, and so I ran. (*Closing his eyes.*) And I ran,
   and I ran, and I ran, and I ran... until I finally got to my momma's
   house. When I got there, she was cooking some *carne. Carne con
   huevos, carne con papas, carne a la carte, carne* kabob, *carne
   con chile, carne* light, and especially *carne con* shrimp. That's all I have
   to say about that. I remember the day that two young boys stopped
   me and took my bicycle from me. They went ahead and broke my
   handlebars, frame, chain, seat, and everything else on that bike. They
   had a lot of hatred, they did. I remember taking my bike back to the
   house, and I had to rebuild it. I did what I could with
   that bike rebuilding it with absolutely no help. (*Low-
   rider music comes on and* Bosque *pulls out his low-rider
   bike from behind the bench. He rides it around a bit.*) After that,
   everyone wanted to have a bike like mine. Soon everyone was riding

them all over the streets and it inspired a few new magazines for the local liquor stores: Low-rider Bike, Bikes That Are Low-Riders, Bikes That Were Not Low-Riders But Now Are, Más Low-Rider Bikes and How Low Can Your Bike Go Magazine. That's all I have to say about that.

HIPPIE 1: (Hippies *walk on stage.*) Ask him his name.

HIPPIE 2: No, you ask him.

HIPPIE 1: Hey, Chicano dude, what's your name, man? Hey man, like, what's your name?

HIPPIE 2: Hey, are you, like, *menso* or something?

BOSQUE: *Menso* is as *menso* does.

HIPPIE 1: That was pretty good, Chicano dude. Hey man, you're pretty smart. You want to join our student organization?

HIPPIE 2: Yeah man, we're Chicano students starting an organization for Chicano students. We just don't have a name yet.

HIPPIE 1: I just got it, man. The name of our organization! It just came to me, man. *Mano.* Why don't we call ourselves *Mano*?

HIPPIE 2: Hey, hey, keep your hands to yourself.

BOSQUE: No thank you, but I'm glad I mecha.

HIPPIE 2: Mecha! Wow, that was so brilliant, Chicano brother. Brilliant! Mecha, get it like a match.

HIPPIE 1: We'll call ourselves M.E.Ch.A: I got it, *Moviemento Estudantil Chicano de Aztlán.* M.E.Ch.A. Wow, that blew my *chonies* off man. (*They go to shake* Bosque's *hand and he does the Chicano handshake.*)

HIPPIE 2: Awesome handshake, brother. (*They exit stage.*)

BOSQUE: After that, M.E.Ch.A groups began to spring up all over the United States. Cal State LA M.E.Ch.A, San Diego State M.E.Ch.A. They even started M.E.Ch.A at Harvard. Everyone then started to use my handshake. Someone named it the Chicano hand shake. That's all I have to say about that. (Bosque *freezes* and *you hear an* Announcer *speak.*)

ANNOUNCER: *Tia Trucha Magazine* gives it ten trucha points. *Low-rider Magazine* gives it—zip, zip, zip—five hydraulics up. *El Pollo Loco* gives it a left over bean burrito and a large coke. Coming to a theatre near youuuu, Bosqueeeeeeeee Gummmmp Gump Gump.

(*End of* acto.)

parody a lo Chicano

65

JORGE RESORTES
By Macedonio Arteaga Jr.

CHARACTERS:

JORGE RESORTES - Host of the show, around fifty years-old, wearing a sports coat with jeans and sneakers. Holding a microphone.

DOÑA SONRISA - A woman in her fifties wearing an apron.

DOÑA REDONDA - A woman in her fifties, wearing a long skirt and a *reboso*. Also has a cardboard circle inside of her blouse that makes her look round.

RICKY - Son of Doña Redonda. A teenage boy, dressed hip, walks and talks cool.

LOLA - Daughter of Doña Sonrisa. Also a teenager, dressed trendy.

ESTEBAN CRUZ - Security guard who keeps everything in order.

AUDIENCE MEMBER - A Puerto Rican with a heavy accent.

SIGN HOLDER- An individual who holds up signs for the audience to respond to.

(*Four chairs are center stage.*)

JORGE: (*Enters.*) Hello, hello, and welcome to our show today where family and friends' secrets become national *chisme*. You all know my name, Jorge Resortes and here to my left, the man who keeps everything in order, Esteban Cruz. (Esteban *flexes his muscles.*) Okay ladies and gentlemen, in order to help our ratings we need your support. Our lovely assistant will be holding up signs. Your job will be to read the signs loudly. Let's practice a little just to assure we're all working together for the network.

SIGN HOLDER: (*Holds up sign* ORALE. *The entire audience says* orale.)

JORGE: *Orale.* Meaning all right.

SIGN HOLDER: (*Holds up sign* QUE GACHO.)

JORGE: *Que gacho.* Meaning messed up.

SIGN HOLDER: (*Holds up sign* ROBA CHANCLAS.)

JORGE: *Roba chanclas.* To our English audience that would be (*He pauses.*) shoe embezzler.

SIGN HOLDER: (*Holds up sign* CHALE.)

JORGE: Chale that would (*He sounds like a stereotypical white cheerleader.*) like forget about it like oh my god no way. Yes my friends, just one word *CHALE.*

SIGN HOLDER: (*Holds up sign* BRUJA.)

JORGE: *Bruja*, plain and simple, witch. That was great for you non-Spanish speaking people this will give you a great opportunity to learn our language. And if you don't know Spanish, learn. You're in California. All right, all right, let's get this show on the road. Let's bring out our first guest, Doña Sonrisa.

SONRISA: (*Enters stage left and sits down.*) Hello, Jorge.

JORGE: Hello, Doña Sonrisa. How are you doing?

SONRISA: Well, I wish better, Jorge. If I'm on this show, something is wrong.

JORGE: (*Sitting right next to* Doña Sonrisa *with his face inches away from hers.*) Yes, yes, tell us. Tell us what's on your mind.

SONRISA: (*Backs away from* Jorge *but he gets closer.*) Well, Jorge, I'm here because there's something I have to confess. Last year *Chisme Magazine* had a food-eating contest at their annual *Come Como Marrano* Contest.

JORGE: Yes, yes, the "Eat Like a Pig" contest for our English audience. (*Looks directly at the audience.*) And? . . (*Staring straight into her face to the point where it's annoying her.*) Ah come on? You should have no shame. "Eat Like a Pig" contest winners should be very proud, Doña. (*He pushes his nose up and makes a pig noise.*)

parody a lo Chicano

SONRISA: Well, Jorge, I entered a secret *chorizo con huevos* recipe that was not mine.

JORGE: Ahh, don't tell me.

SONRISA: (*Starts breaking down.*) No Jorge, it was my *comadre's* recipe. She left it in my house and I entered it in the contest and won. I feel like a dirty rotten criminal. (*She starts crying.*)

SIGN HOLDER: (*Holds up sign* QUE GACHO.)

JORGE: Yes, you should, Doña Sonrisa. Yes, I would pretty much call you rotten for doing that. By the way, what was the first place prize?

SONRISA: Well, I won a lifetime supply of shoes at *Chanclas* are Us and also free *horchata* every time I eat at any of the local Mariabertos restaurants.

JORGE: So basically you stole a free supply of shoes from *Chanclas* are Us. Gosh, they have some nice *chanclas*.

SIGN HOLDER: (*Holds up sign* ROBA CHANCLAS.)

SONRISA: Yes. I feel terrible. So tonight I'm here to confess.

JORGE: All right, rotten old *vieja*. Well let's bring your *comadre* on. Let's welcome, Doña Redonda!

REDONDA: (*Walks in and sees* Doña Sonrisa *and they hug each other.*) *Hola, comadre.*

SONRISA: *Hola.* How have you been, *comadre*? What have you been doing?

REDONDA: Well you know *comadre* like the kids say keeping it real, down for the hood, backing up the homies.

SONRISA: (*Shocked.*) Now, now *comadre*, don't be set tripping.

JORGE: Wow and for those that don't understand slang, learn. Doña Redonda, you really know what's up. So how did you get that name, Doña Redonda? Or should I say Mrs. Round?

REDONDA: Just a nickname really not sure how I got it.

JORGE: So can you tell us? Why did you bring this lovely round lady here?

REDONDA: Yea, *comadre*. Why did you bring me here?

SONRISA: *Comadre*, I actually have a confession to make. I felt the only way I could do it was by coming on this show.

JORGE: Yes, she has a serious confession. Tell her rotten old lady.

SONRISA: Could you please stop calling me that? I feel terrible already about what I'm going to say.

JORGE: Sorry *bruja*.

SIGN HOLDER: (*Holds up sign* BRUJA.)

REDONDA: *Digame, comadre.* We've been through a lot. Nothing you can tell me can ruin our friendship.

SONRISA: Well, *comadre*, I, well, I . . . Remember when I won that contest in *Chisme Magazine*?

REDONDA: Oh, yes I remember you won and you got a lifetime supply of shoes to *Chanclas* are Us. Man, they make some great *chanclas*. What a dream come true!

SONRISA: Yes, well, *comadre*. I entered a *chorizo* recipe that won, but there was one little problem, *comadre*. The *huevos con chorizo* recipe that

Teatro Izcalli

68

I entered was. . . was yours, *comadre*. I'm so sorry. (*Stands up, turns to the side facing the opposite direction of her* comadre *and bites on knuckles, freezing for a couple of seconds in a very dramatic fashion. She then turns back and looks at her* comadre.)

REDONDA: *Comadre*, it's okay. I understand you know good cooking when you smell it, taste it and then steal it. (*Begins to raise her voice.*) Well, I have something to tell you, *bruja*. Remember how you asked me to make your daughter's quinceañera dress. Well, I never made the dress. I bought it at the swap meet.

SIGN HOLDER: (*Holds up sign CHALE.*)

JORGE: You bought the dress at the swap meet. *Miserable*.

SONRISA: (*Gets up and screams.*) ¡Vieja asquerosa! I hope you gain two hundred more pounds. (*Stands on one leg and makes a karate sound. Doña Redonda attacks her and they grab each other by the hair. They're screaming at each other and Esteban jumps in and separates them. They sit down, and he sits in between them.*)

JORGE: Okay, okay. Let's all get a hold of our selves. We still have some surprises left in the show and I would hate to see someone get hurt, even though it would help our ratings. Let's hear from some audience members to see what they have to say. (*Walks up to anybody in the audience and asks them for their opinion. He thanks them for their comments and then he goes to the* Audience Member *who's from the theatre group.*)

AUDIENCE MEMBER: *Yo pienso que tu* ... (*Pointing to* Doña Sonrisa.) *eres una desgraciada. Eres una bestia, coño. ¿Como pudiste hacer eso? Dios mío. Un animal no le hace eso a sus propias amigas. No lo puedo creer.*

JORGE: *Gracias*. Thanks for your opinion. Well, ladies and gentlemen, I have another surprise guest waiting to come on stage. Let's hear it for Lola, the daughter of Doña Sonrisa.

LOLA: (*Enters holding an ugly yellow dress. She walks straight to* Doña Redonda.) I can't believe you actually bought this nasty dress at the swap meet! My quinceañera was supposed to be the most memorable day of my life and it was, but for all the wrong reasons. Nobody's going to forget this ugly dress I had to wear. My chambelan couldn't even find a cumberbun to match it. (*She throws the dress at* Doña Redonda. *Then she tackles her and they both fall to the ground.* Doña Sonrisa *tries to pull her off but she can't.*)

SONRISA: She's not worth it, *mija*. She's not worth it. (Esteban *breaks them up and they all sit down.*)

parody a lo Chicano

JORGE: Aren't you ashamed, Lola? Lola, Lola, low life attacking your own *madrina*. Well, we have to move on. Let's bring out our last guest. Our last guest, ladies and gentlemen, has been in the middle of all this and is in a very difficult situation because he's the boyfriend of Lola and also the son of Doña Redonda. Let's bring out Ricky.

RICKY: (*Enters stage left.*) *Qvole*, it's like this. It's like this. (*He walks past* Doña Sonrisa *and* Lola.) What up? What up? (*He then goes up to* Doña Redonda *and hugs her.*) It's like this, yo. It's like this. Check it out.

JORGE: I don't mean to sound rude, Ricky, but can you say a whole sentence? Or can you tell us why you're here today?

RICKY: *Simon*, it's like this. It's like this. Check it out. Me and my girl, you know, we have been, you know, *tu sabaes*.

JORGE: Very good, Ricky, you almost said a whole sentence. You and your girl have been in love? (*Looks at audience and whispers.*) How did this *baboso* get on my show? (*Goes back to* Ricky.) And why are you here?

RICKY: (*He walks over to* Lola *and gets down on one knee.*) Yo, yo, check it out. Will you, like yo, you know what up, girl, *tu sabes*.

LOLA: Yes, yes, I will. You know, I will.

REDONDA: Don't do it! No! (Doña Redonda *jumps on* Ricky's *back.* Esteban *pulls her off and* Ricky *grabs* Lola's *hand.*)

LOLA: I thought this day would never come.

RICKY: Yo! Yo! It's like this… (*They both exit.*)

(*The* comadres *hug and they're both crying. They exit the stage.*)

JORGE: Life comes down to many things. *Chorizo* is one of them. *Chorizo*, left over cow intestines, eyes, guts, nalgas, feet, the whole thing all-grinded into one. *Chorizo*, should it get in the way of your *comadre's* relationship? The *comadre* who has cleaned your *niños' mocos*, helped you make that *posole* and *tamales* on those late holiday nights. It shouldn't. *Quinceañera* dresses should not be bought at swap meets. If you're only seventeen years old and can't speak in whole sentences, don't ask someone to marry you. And if someone asks you to marry them and they can't speak in whole sentences, don't marry them. This is Jorge Resortes asking you to take care of yourself and others. We look forward to seeing what *chisme* awaits us for next week. *Buenas noches.*

(*End of* acto.)

Teatro Izcalli

70

This *acto* is based on the movie Napolean Dynamite. Like many others, when I first saw the movie I couldn't stop laughing. In this movie, a Mexican played a main character and he wasn't a drug dealer or a gang member. Pedro was an everyday Mexican boy who was struggling within American culture. It made us so happy to see this on the big screen. In the movie Pedro runs for school president and to the surprise of many, he wins. In this *acto* we took that character and had him run for President of the United States. I have a friend, Gabriel "Shaggy" Nuñez who looks like Napolean so I asked him if he wanted to perform in this *acto*. We first performed this *acto* at the MAAC Community Charter School and it was filmed by KPBS since we were being honored for our work in the community.

VOTE FOR PEDRO
By Macedonio Arteaga Jr.

CHARACTERS:

PEDRO - Wearing jeans, white dress shirt, a sports coat, cowboy boots, and a wig.
NAPOLEAN - Wearing jeans, ski boots, and a t-shirt that say's Vote for Pedro.
CHONCHO - Pedro's body guard. Mexican wrestler wearing a mask.

(Choncho *walks on stage followed by* Pedro. *"Hail to the Chief" music plays as* Pedro *approaches the podium*.)

PEDRO: Hello my name is Pedro. I decided to run for President of the United States or somesing. But first I want to thank my bodyguard, Choncho.
CHONCHO: (*Makes a funny high pitched sound*.) Hea, hea.
PEDRO: Choncho is currently on the *carne asada* diet. *Carne asada* in the morning, *carne asada* at lunch, *carne asada* for dinner and *un frego de*

parody a lo Chicano

71

Pepto-Bismol at night. Right, Choncho?

CHONCHO: (*Makes funny high-pitched sound again.*) Hea, hea.

PEDRO: I don't know why Choncho does that. Anyhow I have a lot of changes I want to change. For example, I'm concerned about our health care. So I've decided if you vote for me, you'll get a year supply of *vaporoo*. (*Holds up jar of vaporub.*) My *tia* says it cures a thousand diseases or somesing. She also says if you can't sleep at night, you put it on your eyes and it helps you fall asleep. I sink it'll work. I have some more changes I want to change. I have traveled to many elementary schools and the water always tastes nasty in the drinking fountains. So when I become president, I will change the drinking fountains of America. When you go to drink water you'll have a choice of *horchata* or *tamarindo*. I sink it'll work. Another thing I want to change is that there are too many words that Mexicans can't say in English. So I'm going to change that. For example we can't say regularrrllly. From now on instead of saying regularrrrlly all we have to say is *orale*. For example, I *orale* go to the store to buy *tortillas*. I sink it'll work. Another word we have trouble saying is horrrroorrr. For example, I went to see a horrrrroorrr movie, so from now on instead of saying horrrroorr, we're going to say *cucuy*. For example, I went to see a *cucuy* movie and it escared the nachos out of me. I sink it'll work. (Napolean *walks in rubbing his eyes.*) What's wrong with your eyes?

NAPOLEAN: I couldn't sleep last night so I put *vaporoo* on my eyes like your *tia* said and my eyes are freakin burning. Gossh!

PEDRO: Did you fall asleep?

NAPOLEAN: No, it didn't even work. Gosh!

PEDRO: How come you're late?

NAPOLEAN: George Lucas called me. He said he was impressed with my numb chuck skills. He said he wanted me to be in his next Star Wars movie. He wants me to play Chewbaca. (*Makes a Chewbacca noise.*)

PEDRO: You sound just like him. Oh, did you bring our campaign eslogan? (Napolean *hands* Pedro *a drawing of a half tiger and half chupacabras.*) This is our campaign eslogan. It's a Chuiger. It's a cross between a *chupacbras* and a tiger. I sink it'll work. So this year when you go to the polls vote for Pedro and your wildest dreams will come true. Vote for Pedro. (*He exits the stage.*)

NAPOLEAN: (*Music comes on and he dances. Exits stage before music ends.*

Teatro Izcalli (*End of* acto.)

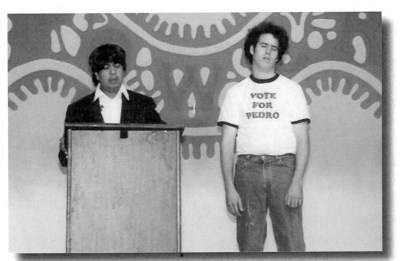

Vote for Pedro, 2006. Macedonio Arteaga Jr. and Gabriel Nuñez.
Photo by Miguel-Angel Soria.

REAL REAL STORIES
OF THE
HIGHBÜEY PATROL
By Teatro Izcalli

CHARACTERS:

CHURRO - Dressed like a tagger, wearing baggy clothes, carrying a spray can.
MACHACA - Dressed very similar to Churro and carrying a spray can.
OFFICER BOB - Officer, narrating the event, dressed like a cop.
DEMO-COP - Wearing a cop uniform, acts out what Officer Bob says. Has a small car and a large doughnut.
SEÑORA VENDEDORA - Carrying a box that she uses to sell items out of.

(Officer Bob *walks onto stage.*)

Teatro Izcalli   OFFICER BOB: Good evening and *buenas noches* to you all. My name is Officer Bob Jones of the Highway Patrol. Welcome to the Real, Real, Real, for Real-we ain't lying-Stories of the Highway Patrol. (*He smiles and his teeth are black from* *chewing tobacco.*) You know, the job of an officer is always dangerous in the high crime areas of Hispanic descent communities. This is where our next story will take us, to the deadly, violent, frightening, terrifying, streets of Barrio Logan. Okay. Let's go to an incident, where I personally lived it. (*Person walks across the stage with a sign that says "Dramatization." Demo-Cop comes in behind him/her in a small police car, eating a large doughnut. Demo-Cop gets out of car and does a quick little dance and makes a pig sound.*)

OFFICER BOB: On October 12th of 1992, exactly five hundred years after we had landed on this here continental breakfast we named America. I was patrolling the predominately Hispanic Indian-looking community of Barrio Logan, where the residents have a loving and respectful relationship with yours truly. (*Demo-Cop is in his car eating his doughnut.* Señora Vendedora *walks by.*)

SEÑORA VENDEDORA: *Señoras, vengan para aca les tengo un remedio que es puro milagro. Un milagro les digo. Mire, si a su esposo no se le para. Pero oiganme bien. Si a su esposo no se le para ... LA TOZ. Dele usted este remedio de ...* (*She's selling cough syrup from her box.*)

OFFICER BOB: I noticed a resident selling confiscated illegal Indian remedies without a permit. I asked her in the Hispanic Indian cultural language if she had a permit for the holistic product she was perpetuating.

DEMO COP: *¿Tu tener permiso para sus nalgas?*

OFFICER BOB: Since she did not answer, I was then forced to give her a minor violation ticket for selling undocumented illegal alien material without a legal permit with intent to sell. (*Demo-Cop throws her box on the ground and kicks it.*)

OFFICER BOB: She responded positively to my warning and informed me she would be getting a permit very soon. (*He laughs.*)

SEÑORA VENDEDORA: (*Picks up her stuff and yells at him.*) *¡Hijo de la gran caca!* (*Storms off stage.*)

OFFICER BOB: Two hours later, as I was wrapping up my report which I titled, "The Selling Permit Incident". I noticed out of the corner of my eye two hoodlums of the Hispanic persuasion deflamating private property.

CHURRO: (Churro *and* Machaca *are painting a mural with spray cans.*) *¿Que onda, Machaca?* What do you think loco? (*He points to the wall.*)

MACHACA: That looks sick, Churro. *Está enfermo,* man.

parody a lo Chicano

OFFICER BOB: I approached them cautiously and calmly. (*Demo-Cop rolls on the ground and then snorts like a pig.*) As I noticed the

75

Hispanic Indian-looking characters, I politely asked them what they were doing.

DEMO-COP: What do you beaners think you're doing?

MACHACA: Nothing man, nothing.

CHURRO: Nothing.

OFFICER BOB: You know the life of an officer is always at stake and we must always react with animal-like reflexes. (Demo-Cop *squeals*.) That evening I was very aware that I was outnumbered so I had to act quickly. I recall telling them to hold their hands up high and not cause any problems.

DEMO-COP: If any of youz ugly beaners move, I'll execute every last one of you!

OFFICER BOB: In that instant, one of the assailants attacked me with an evil Aztec kick. (Churro *slips on spray can and farts*.) And a deadly gas was omitted. (Demo-Cop *holds his breath and* Churro *gets up*.) I knew my life was in danger, so I fired two warning shots in the air. (Demo-Cop *shoots with a gun but you hear a machine gun sound. He hits* Machaca.)

MACHACA: (*Starts spinning on one leg*.) You shot my leg! You shot my leg! (*He pauses and looks at the audience*.) I'm telling my mom. (*He falls to the ground*. Churro *yells and grabs his friend, trying to revive him*. Churro *tugs on* Machaca's *shoe and the shoe comes off. It smells really bad*. Churro *circles around as if he's about to pass out*.)

OFFICER BOB: The other suspect attacked me with a concealed weapon, but he realized he was out weaponed. The suspect took off running. Unfortunately, I suffered a minor set back and needed to call for back up.

DEMO-COP: (Demo-Cop *starts to run but he drops the doughnut he's been holding the whole time. He dives to the ground to pick it up and speaks into walkie talkie*.) Officers' doughnut down! Officers' doughnut down! Requesting back up, repeat doughnut down! (*Picks up his doughnut and eats it*.)

OFFICER BOB: I then gave an adequate description of the suspect.

DEMO-COP: Roger, roger, three little lambs, and jack in a beanstalk, over. I have one Machaca down and a Churro who ran for the border. He's a brown male between four and six feet tall, of the Hispanic Indian cultural descent, wearing baggy clothes, and has long hair. Suspect is armed and dangerous. Repeat armed and dangerous.

OFFICER BOB: Raúl Sánchez Roquerario de Espirito Santo, A.K.A. Machaca, was charged with assault with a deadly weapon, second degree attempted murder, 1st degree black belt homicide, 3-D battery, and failure to stop at a stop sign. He's currently serving 99 to 149 years in the state penitentiary.

Teatro Izcalli

76

The second suspect a Mario Herendido Torres Denalga, otherwise known as Churro, was caught at a local swap meet two hours later. He was charged with 1st degree attempted cow slaughter, resisting arrest, resisting to subscribe to cable TV, carrying a concealed weapon, wearing butt-huggers, and armed burglary. He's facing his second strike in our newly built prison very close to where the scene took place. For myself, Officer Bob Jones, I was given the highest medal for bravery and was given a free paid vacation to Guadalajara, Mexico to learn more about the beautiful Mexican culture. *Señoritas and margaritas.* Yeah! That's all for this week's segment. We'll see you all next week in the next episode of the Real, Real, Real, for real —we ain't lying — Stories of the Highway Patrol.

(Ends with the "Cops" music in the background.)

1996. Left to right: Abel Macias, Benny Madera, Olympia Rodriguez, Victor Chavez Jr., Maria Santos, Alicia Chavez, Macedonio Arteaga Jr., Alejandro Ochoa.

parody a lo Chicano

A
   Chicano
      Seinfeld
         skit.
  About
     nothing
       but
         everything.

DROPPED TORTILLA
By Macedonio Arteaga Jr. & Alicia Chavez

CHARACTERS:

Modeled after Seinfeld TV Show
ELENA - In her thirties, wearing glasses and a business suit.
JERRY - Tall and thin, speaks slowly. Wearing jeans and a t-shirt.
JORGE - Bald, chubby, and wearing glasses.
KRAMER - Messy hair, wearing retro clothes and jittery.

(Jorge *sitting at a table with 4 chairs.* Jerry *enters.*)

JERRY: Hey, Jorge.
JORGE: I did it man. I dropped it. Boom just like that. Yep. I was
    reaching over to give her the engagement ring, Jer, and I dropped it.
        JERRY: Dropped what?
`Teatro Izcalli`   JORGE: I dropped the *tortilla* on the ground.
        JERRY: You did what??!!!
JORGE: Dropped it, Jerry, the *tortilla*, on the ground. She ran out
    screaming, slapped me first… slapped me right here. (*Pointing to*

78

his cheek.) It was just a *tortilla*, Jer. It was just a *tortilla*.

JERRY: On the day you were going to ask her to marry you? You know, my great grandfather once dropped a *tortilla*.

JORGE: What are you talking about? It was just a *tortilla*!

JERRY: It's not JUST a *tortilla*. Can you imagine if every Mexican man would just drop a *tortilla* and nobody would say anything? What would happen to our culture?

KRAMER: (*Enters stage stumbling.*) I know what you did buddy. Yeah. You're in big trouble now. Jer, did he tell you?

JERRY: Yep.

KRAMER: You should have just told her that you didn't want to marry her, instead of dropping a *tortilla* in her presence. That's a crime you know. It's a crime! You're in big trouble.

JORGE: She slapped me.

KRAMER: She should have done a lot more than that. She should have called them.

JORGE: Called who?

ELENA: (*Enters.*) Hey guys. I've got news.

JERRY: About your boyfriend, I'm guessing.

ELENA: Yep. I dumped him. He's gone. Out of my life. Dummmpppeed him.

JERRY: There's a lot of dumping going on.

ELENA: I left him, and you won't believe why? He flushed the toilet before he was done peeing. Yeah. I heard him. He was still peeing and then he flushed the toilet. If a man cannot wait to flush before he's officially done, then I don't want any part of him.

JERRY: That's serious. You've got to flush when you're done, not during.

KRAMER: But did you check to see if all the pee was gone?

JERRY: It shouldn't matter. He tried to beat the flush!

ELENA: Yeah, if he can't wait to flush until he's done, then I don't want to be with him.

KRAMER: I never wait, never ever wait. I just get too anxious watching it come out. Plus I kind of like to race the flush. You know get everything out before the flush. It's a rush! Yeah!

JERRY: You gotta wait. You don't race the flush. That's irresponsible. It's immature.

KRAMER: Some guys are like that buddy, ok?

ELENA: (*Looks at* Jorge.) And how come you're not talking?

JORGE: I dropped a *tortilla* at the restaurant last night.

ELENA: Wait! (*Points at him.*) That was you! parody a lo Chicano

KRAMER: Oh yeah! You're in big trouble, buddy, big trouble. I'm calling them. (*Starts to leave and stops to grab the* tortillas *on the table.*) I'm taking these *tortillas*, buddy. Yeah, I'm not letting you drop these. No way. That's serious...you...you...*tortilla* dropper! (*Mumbling as he walks away.*) I'm calling them right now.

JORGE: Who? What is he talking about?

JERRY: He isn't going to call them.

ELENA: Oh, he will call them.

JORGE: Cally wally. I don't know what you're all talking about!

ELENA: So have you told your parents?

JORGE: Told them what!!??

JERRY: That you dropped it. You know, the *tortilla*?

ELENA: Your parents don't know?! Your mom's going to be very disappointed in her Jorgito. What a shame. It's a crime in some places.

JORGE: Now let me see? What you're telling me is... that because I dropped a *tortilla* in a restaurant, a woman slaps me before I ask her to marry me and now I'm a criminal?

JERRY: You're a criminal.

JORGE: Rush Limbaugh is promoting racial hatred and I'm a criminal for dropping a *tortilla*! No woman has the right to slap a man for dropping a *tortilla*. For goodness sake, Hitler was a criminal. Christopher Columbus was a criminal. I'm not a criminal. I just dropped a *tortilla*!

ELENA: You know Jorge...I once knew a guy who dropped a *tortilla* at a *quinceañera*. He caught it in mid air, it didn't hit the ground and that was it. It was too late. It was over.

JERRY: Yea... they called them.

JORGE: They called who?

ELENA: They called them.

JORGE: For goodness sake, it was just a *tortilla*.

ELENA: Did you say it was just a *tortilla*?

JORGE: Yes!

JERRY: That's what the guy said, that it was just a tortilla before...

ELENA: Oh I don't want to be here when they show up.

(Jerry and Elena *look at each other oddly and they both leave quickly.*)

JORGE: Who? Who? Hey, where are you going? (*Yelling.*) It was just a *tortilla*!

Teatro Izcalli (*End of* acto.)

CHEERLEADERS
By Macedonio Arteaga Jr. and Cristina Nuñez

CHARACTERS:

POPOCATEPTL - First Chicano male cheerleader in the history of the United States. Named after the volcano legend in Mexico. Friends and family call him Popo for short. Dressed as a cheerleader.

IZTACCIHUATL - Named after the volcano next to Popocateptl. She never made the cheerleading squad in high school and ended up sueing the school for racial discrimination. Unfortunately she lost because 93.5% of the cheerleaders were of Mexican descent. Friends call her Iztac for short. Dressed as a cheerleader.

COW - Person in a cow costume.

(Popo *and* Iztac *walk on stage.*)

IZTAC: Look Popo it looks like M.E.Ch.A is preparing for the *carne asada* fundraiser.

POPO: How do you know that's what they're doing?

parody a lo Chicano

IZTAC: Because they're chasing the cow with knives in their hands, that should tell you something.

POPO: Oh wow. So that's what a cow really looks like outside of a burrito. (*La Vaca song comes on by Mala Fe. Cow runs across the stage, dancing and mooing.*)

IZTAC: Oh no Popo, the cow got away. Now M.E.Ch.A can't have a *carne asada* fundraiser. How are they going to raise money now to support the struggle?

POPO: Yea, I struggle to get up in the morning and sometimes when I'm constipated I struggle to... (*Puts her hand over his mouth and interupts him.*)

IZTAC: Nobody needs to know about that struggle. They're talking about another struggle.

POPO: OK I understand but here's another struggle. I'm struggling to see why we're not doing a *carne asada* fundraiser cheer for M.E.Ch.A?

IZTAC: Well the *carne* just left the *asada*, Popo.

POPO: Yea you're right, but wait, wait, I have an idea. They could have a vegeterian *carne asada taco* sale!

IZTAC: Popo, it would just be a vegeterian *taco* if there's no *carne asada* in it.

POPO: Wait, wouldn't we be lying to people if we called it a vegeterian *carne asada taco*? This is too much for my brain to think about. Brain overload. Brain overload. (*Popo freezes in an awkward pose.*)

IZTAC: Oh no. I sure hate doing this but I have too. (*She slaps Popo.*)

POPO: (*He snaps out of it.*) Thanks Iztac, I kind of froze up. Where were we?

IZTAC: We're going to do a cheer for the the vegeterian *carne asada taco* sale.

POPO: Oh yea.

IZTAC: Well let's stop struggling and do it.

IZTAC: It started as a *vaca*, you know it as a cow.

POPO: They tried to go prepare it so that we could chow.

IZTAC: They have black and whites spots and look very round.

POPO: Mooo mooo moo moo is how they sound.

IZTAC This one got away.

POPO: Far far far away.

IZTAC: We still have *guacamole, salsa,* and some beans.

POPO: We will have the fundraiser by any *pinche* means.

IZTAC: We throw on some *tortillas* and flip them until
Teatro Izcalli they're ready. (*Pause.*)

POPO: Flip flip flip the *tortilla*!

IZTAC: Yea yea yea!

POPO: Vegeterian *carne asada* fundraiser!!!

82

IZTAC: Two *tacos* for five dollars.

POPO: Yea yea yea!! Or ten *tacos* for three dollars!

POPO: Oh my god, Iztac, I'm so excited. I feel so empowered.

IZTAC: Popo, you don't even know what that means but it made sense I feel it also.

POPO: I really made sense, Iztac? Wow, now I'm motivated to do the perfect cheer.

IZTAC: Oh my god Popo, you have used two big words in a row.

POPO: Yea. I feel it, Iztac. This is like an oxymoron. Yea yea.

IZTAC: All right Popo that made no sense what so ever. Actually it kind of makes some weird sense, now that I think about it. Anyhow, you know what time it is?

POPO and IZTAC: Time for the perfect cheer! (*Perfect cheer is a choreographed dance to music. At end of dance, they jump around.*) Yea M.E.Ch.A! Vegeterian *carne asada*! Yea, two for a dollar. Extra *guacamole*!

POPO: We did it Iztac! We did it. There's no way M.E.Ch.A can find someone else who is better than us. I know they'll ask us to cheer at all of their events. Yea! (*They exit stage screaming.*)

(*End of* acto.)

Teatro Izcalli

El Movimento

Teatro Izcalli

LATINO seemed sour
HISPANIC bitter
MEXICAN AMERICAN salty
CHICANO/A a mouth watering experience of SELF-DETERMINATION.

~Macedonio Arteaga Jr.

CHICANAS ON TELEVISON
By Macedonio Arteaga Jr.

CHARACTERS:

MOM & DAD - Both are older, in their fifties.
LUCHITA - Twelve years old.

Props: Couch, television, laundry basket.

(Luchita *is watching television and* Mom's *doing laundry.*)
LUCHITA: Wait a second. Is that what I think it is? (*She gets closer to the television.*) Oh my god. It can't be. No way. I think it is. *Mamí, papí,* run! Run! You're not going to believe this! There's a Chicana on television!
MOM: Is it Edward James Olmos?
LUCHITA: No, mom. A Chicana not a Chicano. Run! Run! There's a Chicana on television!
MOM: (*Drops basket of laundry.*) *Viejo! Viejo,* run! There's a Chicana on television.
DAD: (*Runs on stage.*) There's a Chicana on television? (*Picks up his cell phone.*) *Compadre,* listen. Listen, man. There's

el movimiento

a Chicana on television. I don't know what channel yet. What channel, Luchita? (*Urgently.*) What channel?

LUCHITA: Channel 13, *papí*. Channel 13.

DAD: *Canal 13. Canal 13.* Okay, bye. I'll call you later.

MOM: She looks Chicana. She's playing a maid.

LUCHITA: She has an accent.

DAD: Did you hear that? Did you hear that? She said, "No way, José." Wow, another Chicana on television.

MOM: (*Looks like she's going to cry.*) I'm getting very emotional. "Yes, sir, I'll wash that." What a great line.

LUCHITA: Mom, I always wanted to be like you when I grow up. Please don't feel bad, but I want to be like her someday. I want to be on a television show and be a maid.

MOM: Oh, *mija*, that's okay. I won't take it personal.

DAD: Wait here come the credits. Let's find out if she's… there it is. Maid played by Angela Linguini.

MOM & DAD: Oh, she's Italian.

LUCHITA: She might be part Mexican though. She had a good accent. She might be part Mexican.

MOM: *Mija*, it's okay. Let's try not to force it.

DAD: *Mija*, someday we'll produce our own television show and you'll be a great actress. Okay, *mija*?

LUCHITA: All right, daddy.

(*End of* acto.)

Teatro Izcalli

When we first started Teatro Izcalli, we had thrown this idea around of writing a skit about activists from our community in a rehabilitation session. We talked and joked about it and never wrote the *acto* for many years. Finally in 2001, I sat down and wrote the first draft of Chicano Rehab. That same year in March in front of eight hundred people we first performed it at the National M.E.Ch.A conference to a standing ovation. With time the sketch evolved as Claudia Cuevas, Iyari Arteaga, Tina Nuñez, and Alicia Chavez added some lines as they performed their characters on stage. After years of performing the *acto* and working with Jorge Huerta, we finalized what is now known as Chicano Rehab Center. Chicano Rehab Center is a look at our selves and the passion we have as activists. After we perform this *acto*, we always have people ask us if a character was based on them since they can relate to it so much.

CHICANO REHAB CENTER
By Macedonio Arteaga Jr. & Teatro Izcalli

CHARACTERS:

COUNSELOR - Dressed like Frida Khalo, even has a monkey on her shoulder, eyebrows look like Frida's.

RAÚL MUCHASARMAS - Old Chicano activist who is dressed in camouflage clothes. Raul thinks that the only way to liberate our people is through armed revolution.

SUSANNA ODIAHOMBRES - Chicana feminist, who's very wary of men and their actions. Wearing jeans and a motorcycle leather jacket. Has a sword stashed in her jacket.

CRISTINA ESTUDIANADA - Wearing a college sweatshirt with a backpack.

MOCTEZUMA - Spiritual Indian who believes ceremony is the only way to liberate the people. Talks very slowly. Has a coyote skin covering his body and is wearing a taparabos, also wearing necklaces and a bandana on his head.

JOEL - Dressed like Diego Rivera, wearing overalls with el movimiento paint on them.

NOTE: The characters are sitting in the following order: First the Counselor, next Susanna, then Moctezuma, followed by Raúl, and then Cristina.

(*All of the characters enter the stage.* Estudianada *and* Odiahombres *sit on their chairs, but* Muchasarmas *puts his chair down and lays down behind it.* Moctezuma *sits on the ground as if he's meditating.* Joel *then enters stage holding a clipboard. After everyone is seated, the* Counselor *walks in.*)

COUNSELOR: Diego, why don't you have your brushes? (Joel *looks at her frustrated.*)

JOEL: What are you talking about? My name is not Diego. It's Joel. Don't you think you're taking this Frida Khalo thing a bit too far?

COUNSELOR: What are you talking about? Listen if you're going to work for me, you need to wear the proper dress code, Diego. Go paint a mural or something.

JOEL: My name is not Diego! Uhhhggg! (*He exits stage frustrated.*)

COUNSELOR: My god, that man has problems. Maybe he should be in our sessions? All right everyone, welcome to Chicano Rehab Center. As you all know, you're here. . . Excuse me, would you please sit on your chairs? (Muchasarmas *and* Moctezuma *sit on their chairs.*) Yes, thank you. All right, as I was saying, you're all here because you got to the point where you've became obsessed with being a Chicano-slash-Chicana. Some of you were referred by a friend, wife, husband, neighbor, or an FBI agent. However, you're all in this room for the same reason: your obsession with trying to out Chicano slash Chicana the world. Now in order to get started with the session, I'm going to ask that you put your weapons, means of communication, or sharp objects on the floor. We'll start here with Cristina, I believe your name is. (Estudianada *leaves her cell phone in the middle of the stage.*)

MUCHASARMAS: (*Gets up and talks on a walkie talkie.*) *Cuauhtli nahui, cuauhtli nahui,* come in *cuauhtli nahui.* Message to all troops: I will be disengaging for several hours. Please relocate to code fourteen *iztac cuauhtli.* Repeat: relocate to code fourteen *iztac cuauhtli.* (*He then takes out a gun, a pager, cell phones, a grenade, and a rocket launcher he carries on his back.*) Never know when you're going to need a rocket launcher with this oppressive system breathing down your neck. OK my counsel, I'm all yours for the next fifteen hundred hours. (*He rolls then crawls as if he's going under barbed wire back to his seat.*)

COUNSELOR: Thank you, Raúl. I know it was hard for you. Next.

Teatro Izcalli MOCTEZUMA: (Moctezuma *gets up and makes an eagle sound and waves his hand to the right then left. Then takes out a cell phone from his bag.*)

MOCTEZUMA: Old school phone. (*Makes the eagle sound and waves his hand to the right then left again. Then sits down.)*

COUNSELOR: Next please.

ODIAHOMBRES: (Odiahombres *takes out her cell phone and sets it down. You can see a sword sticking out of the inside pocket of her jacket.*)

COUNSELOR: Susanna um, could you please leave the sword on the ground? Just for the safety of others.

ODIAHOMBRES: I was taught to never leave my guard down.

COUNSELOR: Susanna, it's going to be okay.

ODIAHOMBRES: (*Stands there thinking about it. She moves towards* Muchasarmas *and* Moctezuma *and points her sword at them.*) If any of you sexist pigs try anything, I'll end your sexist lives right here! (Moctezuma *jumps on* Muchasarma's *lap, scared.*) Do you understand? (*They both nod their heads yes.* Moctezuma *eventually goes back to his seat, slowly.* Susana *walks over and puts her sword down with caution and speaks very nicely to the group.*) Thank you all so much for your support.

COUNSELOR: Okay. I think we're ready to continue. We shall continue the same way we went around. Begin by telling us a bit about yourself. Okay, Miss Estudianada.

ESTUDIANADA: My name is Cristina Estudianada, and I would like to start by saying... I have a problem. I'm a Chicanaholic. I'm addicted to the movement. I'm in my thirteenth year of college. I've been M.E.Ch.A. chair on three separate occasions and I've chaired the national conference twice. I've organized Chicano/a graduation six times and it's really emotional (*Gets teary eyed.*) because it's never been my graduation. I organized the largest M.E.Ch.A. central meeting in the past ten years. I've been President of Associated Students helping to represent the *raza.* (*Speaks as if delivering a speech.*) One of my accomplishments was getting rid of the sellout Hispanic fraternities and sororities at school who don't want to take action on issues that are affecting our people, because they don't want to get political. (*She gets up screaming.*) We wouldn't be in this school if we didn't get political. Nobody will listen to the needs of the underrepresented students of this campus if we're not political. (*The rest of the group is applauding.*) I also organized students to get rid of racist mascots on campus and also. . . (*Gets interrupted.*)

COUNSELOR: Cristina, okay. Thank you. That's what we want to hear. Let it all out. It's important to list your accomplishments. But I have two questions Cristina, or maybe, just one. You've been in college for thirteen years, right? **el movimiento**

ESTUDIANADA: Yes.

COUNSELOR: My records say you have only completed six units. Is that true?

ESTUDIANADA: Yes. That's why I'm here. I've run out of financial aid and my parents will no longer help me pay my rent until I've completed a whole semester. It's just so hard. There are so many injustices on campus that I must fight. It's hard to study. It's hard to study.

MUCHASARMAS: (Raul *puts his arm around her.*) It's okay my little soldier.

ODIAHOMBRES: (*Jumps up, pulls out a screwdriver, and holds it up to* Muchasarma's *neck.* Moctezuma *dives behind* Muchasarma's *chair, afraid.*) Let go of her now and nobody gets hurt! Don't ever touch a woman unless she asks to be touched and even then you better know how and where to touch her!

MUCHASARMAS: (*Shaking. Let go of* Cristina.) Okay, okay. (Moctezuma *gets up, grabs his chair, and pulls it closer to* Muchasarma's. *He's very afraid.* Moctezuma *sprinkles some powder on* Odiahombres *from a distance.*)

COUNSELOR: Everybody please, get a hold of yourself. I know you want to share but part of rehab is to encourage you all to have patience and not cheer anyone on during the session. Next please.

MUCHASARMAS: Raúl Muchasarmas, *a sus ordenes*, my counsel. I believe in demilitarizing the border, taking back *Aztlán*. The only way will be through weapons, lots of weapons. I have been running from the CIA, the FBI, the NWA, NBA for several years now, eluding them like a fox. I started the Brown Berets in the sixties and founded the Chicano Liberation Front. (*He stands up.*) I visited Che Guevara in Mexico and have had breakfast, lunch, and dinner with the greatest leader against capitalism: Fidel Castro. ¡*Que viva la revolución*! (*They all scream,* "¡Que viva!".) *Compañeros*, we must destroy the machine, the machine that destroys the dreams and hopes of our children. We continue to have more people in prison than graduating from college. *Compañeros la revolución* is not over!

COUNSELOR: Raúl, thank you. Raúl! Raúl!

MUCHASARMAS: (*He continues talking.*) The machine is running at full force, and only we can stop it. (*Rambling.*)

COUNSELOR: (*The* Counselor *takes a taco out of her dress and throws it at him.* Muchasarmas *falls to the ground.*) Raul are you ok?

MUCHASARMAS: Yes, that reminded me of the Chicano Moratorium when I got zapped by the *placa*. Wow, what a rush!

COUNSELOR: Sorry I had to resort to those tactics, Raúl but we lost all communication.

MUCHASARMAS: Whatever it takes, my counsel. Whatever it takes.

COUNSELOR: Raúl, you were sent here by your wife. Correct?

MUCHASARMAS: (*Puzzled.*) Wife?

92

COUNSELOR: Yes, Raúl, your wife. You also have two kids.

MUCHASARMAS: Two kids? (*He holds up two fingers.*) Wow, two kids? Two more soldiers for the revolution!

COUNSELOR: Yes, Raúl that's exactly why you are here. We'll come back to you but for right now let's move on. Okay, Moctezuma.

MOCTEZUMA: (*Speaking slowly.*) Relatives, I see the spirits. They're here. I hear them. They speak to me. They say one of you ate at Taco Bell this morning. Ten Mexican pizzas and fifteen tacos for thirty-nine cents, you have betrayed our culture. Today they ask me to speak about something more important. They say an armed struggle got us nowhere in the '60's. This government has tried to destroy our spirits before they established their constitution. Relatives, have they been able to do so? No, I say the spirits of our ancestors are still here. *Welkati to yoytol agee.* (*In the Nahuatl language he's saying, "Guide our hearts and spirits".*) I see them. They're here sitting around us, holding us, guiding us. They say weapons will get us nowhere. They say, listen to the message and principles of our greatest leader César Chávez. He left us ten principles to follow. They say these principles when applied to their fullest capacity can overcome all wrong which is oppressing our people. We must launch the revolution, the revolution of the spirit. We need to rebuild our temples, bring back our ceremonies, and ask for guidance. We must continue the quest for self-sacrifice that leads to spiritual energy that is unstoppable. César and his people were a few, but a revolution with millions can and will be the solution.

COUNSELOR: Moctezuma, okay. Slow down, brother. I feel your message but you're here for the same reason as everyone else. You've taken our traditional ways to an unhealthy level.

MOCTEZUMA: Our traditional ways could never be unhealthy.

COUNSELOR: Moctezuma, you go to three sweat lodges a day. You're in medicine teepee ceremonies every weekend. You do *danza azteca* five days a week and sundance nine times a year, and you haven't made a payment on your credit cards in five years. Your car has been repossessed; you lost your house, your wife, and your mom says you haven't called her in three years.

MOCTEZUMA: I communicate with her in spirit form.

COUNSELOR: Yeah, we all know you can see (*Whispering.*) dead people. You may communicate with them in spirit form but they haven't been able to get a hold of you yet. And your name really isn't Moctezuma. Isn't it Christian?

el movimiento

MOCTEZUMA: (*Screaming.*) Nooooooo!!!!! Noooo!!!

COUNSELOR: Christian! Christian, Christian! It's time Christian for you to wake up and face the truth. We'll come back and continue

93

this discussion later. Now let us move on to Susanna.

ODIAHOMBRES: I speak on behalf of all women. First and foremost, we shall boycott the book *The Surrendered Wife* written by that sellout *mujer* Laura Doyle. There's no way women will go back to give men full power and control of the home and finances. ¡*Chale*! We shall gather her books and recycle them to produce the *Feminist Manifesto: the full liberation of womyn (Changes her tone of voice to a sales pitch.)* which by the way was written by yours truly and will be out this summer. *Mujeres*, we must liberate women from the oppressor. The oppressor: he who has a penis that is the oppressor. (Muchasarmas *and* Moctezuma *cross their legs.*) We shall no longer call them sweetie pies or pumpkin pies but we shall call them for what they are. Oppressors! Oppressors! (Muchasarmas *and* Moctezuma *jerk every time she says oppressors.*) It's because of them that we are living in this misery and pain. We shall not wash one darn *plato* for them. I ask you, do they not have hands? (Muchasarmas *and* Moctezuma *look at their hands.*) *Mujeres*, we must organize. We must mobilize! ¡*Que viva la mujer*!

COUNSELOR: Susanna, thank you for that splendid and vivid speech, especially the part about the pumpkin pie. I'm kinda hungry. Now, Susanna is it not true that last week you were seen hand washing your boyfriend's *calsones*?

ODIAHOMBRES: No. Heck no!

COUNSELOR: Oh no? Is it not true that you were seen rubbing your boy friends feet?

ODIAHOMBRES: (*Breaks down crying.*) But they're so cute (*Ashamed.*)

COUNSELOR: Well, on that note, I want to thank everyone for their words. Now it's time for us to start looking inside our selves. Why can't we let go just a little bit? Who are the people we are hurting instead of helping? This exercise will be painful, but this is the first step to begin discussing the hurt. We'll start with Cristina. Now, Cristina, we have heard of your incredible activism and the contributions you have made to the student movement but I want to start looking deeper inside. (Joel *walks in.*)

JOEL: I know, I'm never to interrupt a session but something very serious has happened...

COUNSELOR: Yes, Diego. (Joel *looks at her and is about to say his name is not* Diego *but he brushes it off.*) Group, take a moment to begin reflecting on the people you are hurting in your lives. (*She goes off to the side with* Joel.) Yes? What happened?

JOEL: The Anti-*Chorizo* Initiative, Prop 22 passed!

COUNSELOR: (*She yells.*) WHAT!!! (*Everyone looks at her.*) Okay, we must remain calm. We're in session. We will deal with this matter

94

when our session is over. Thank you, Diego. (Joel *rolls his eyes and walks out.*) I can't believe this! (*Real calm and then yells the last words.*) Ladies and gentlemen, our greatest fear has just occurred. Prop 22, the Anti-*Chorizo* Initiative has just passed!

EVERBODY: (*Jumping off their chairs together.*) WHAT!!!

COUNSELOR: Everyone sit down and listen. There's a lot of competent people out there who can organize and mobilize against this initiative. We must learn to let go. (*Whispering to the audience.*) What would Frida do? (*She picks up a cell phone and yells.*) ¡Que viva la revolución!

EVERYBODY: ¡¡¡*QUE VIVA*!!! (*As they run out, they say their last line.*)

ESTUDIANADA: (*Picks up cell phone.*) Girl, we need to organize a M.E.Ch.A. meeting.

MUCHASARMAS: (*Picks up walkie talkie.*) *Cuauhtli nahui,* come in *cuauhtli nahui.* Send all troops to region 12. Repeat: all troops to region 12.

MOCTEZUMA: (*Picks up cell phone.*) Light the fire! We need to have a sweat!!!

ODIAHOMBRES: (*Picks up sword.*) I need to call the *mujeres,* because we need our *chorizo!*

JOEL: (*A phone rings.*) Hello, Chicano Rehab Center. No, my name is not Diego!!! No, the counselor is not in. Yep, she relapsed again.

(*End of* acto.)

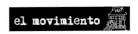

Chicano Rehab Center, 2008. Jose Alvarez
and Macedonio Arteaga Jr.
Photo by Sylvia Romo-Lara.

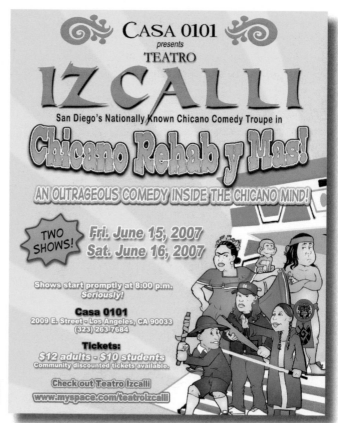

Flyer design by Juan
Carlos Sanchez.
Artwork by Nopalico

Teatro Izcalli

Chicano Starter Kit was written by

Alicia Chavez

Claudia Cuevas

Cristina Nuñez

Three Chicanas

¿y que?

CHICANO STARTER KIT
By Teatro Izcalli

CHARACTERS:

MOM - In her forties, wearing a huipil.
SON - High school age.
ANNOUNCER - Wearing a suit.

Props: Marker, paper, M.E.Ch.A t-shirt with buttons from the Chicano movement, *moral* (bag) for mom, Rage Against the Machine CD, cliff notes, book "Occupied America".

(Mom *is on stage making picket signs.*)
SON: (*Enters stage left.*) Hi, mom. What are you doing?
MOM: Making picket signs for the *marcha* this weekend. (Son *sighs.*) How
    was your day, *mijo*?
SON: *Ay, amá.* It was a disaster. I went to my first
    M.E.Ch.A meeting today and I got kicked out!
    They said I wasn't Chicano enough.

el movimiento

MOM: What? You tell those *mocoso*s your mother has been a Chicana for over thirty years! I marched with César Chávez. I was at the Chicano Moratorium in 1970. Heck, *mijo*, you've been raised on boycotting grapes.

SON: You're right, *amá*. I don't even know what a grape tastes like.

MOM: You know, *mijo*, I always feared this day would come but don't worry. I'm prepared.

SON: What do you have?

MOM: I ordered it from *Galavision*.

SON: The same ones that sell *Inglés Sin Barreras*.

MOM: Yes, mijo, they're really up with the times. Look, *mijo* (*Pulls out a bag.*) your very own "Chicano Starter Kit."

SON: Wow.

MOM: Look, *mijo*. Your Chicano Starter Kit comes with the 30th anniversary edition of the M.E.Ch.A t-shirt. (*She pulls out M.E.Ch.A t-shirt.*) Not only that, but it comes with all the buttons: boycott grapes, don't eat grapes, grapes are bad, and all of the classics No on 187, No on 209, No on 227 and *un indio quiere llorar*. Nobody can say you're not a Chicano wearing this shirt. (*Announcer enters stage left.*)

ANNOUNCER: Do you too have that not-so-Chicano feeling? If you do, you can also have your very own Chicano Starter Kit. If you order now, your Chicano Starter Kit will also come with a CD by Rage Against the Machine, a copy of *Occupied America*, and cliff notes for *El Plan de Santa Barbara*. That's right. You too can own your own Chicano Starter Kit. A $75 value for only four easy payments of $24.99. That's right, four easy payments of $24.99, but wait! If you order within the next thirty minutes, your Chicano Starter Kit will also come with the protest package. The protest package comes with a CD with all the classic Chicano chants such as...

MOM AND SON: (*Marching in place.*) Sí se puede. Sí se puede.

ANNOUNCER: And...

MOM AND SON: (*Fists in the air.*) El pueblo unido jamas será vencido.

ANNOUNCER: And who could forget the interactive Chicano classic...

SON: What do we want?

MOM: Justice!

SON: When do we want it?

MOM: Now!

ANNOUNCER: And as a bonus we've added the

Teatro Izcalli

campesino classic...

MOM AND SON: (*Singing.*) De colores. De colores se visten los campos en la primavera.

ANNOUNCER: So if you call within the next thirty minutes, the protest package will be part of your Chicano Starter Kit but that's not all. Within the next ten minutes, we're slashing prices. That's right. (*Does a karate kick in the air.*) We're knocking them down. You'll only have to make three easy payments of $44.99 and your Chicano Starter Kit will also come with an instructional video on the Chicano handshake. (Mom *and* Son *demonstrate handshake in slow motion.*)

MOM: You finally learned it, *baboso.*

SON: Thank you, mom.

ANNOUNCER: You'll also receive this beautiful upside down Aztec calendar (*Holding a poster of Aztec calender upside down.*) with complete instructions on how to find your indigenous name. You can show off your name to all your friends: Three Deer, *Four Xochitl,* Six *Huaraches,* and many more. So order within the next ten minutes, and you'll only have to make three easy payments of $64.99. So remember...

ANNOUNCER, MOM, and SON: Don't start M.E.Ch.A without it!

(*End of* acto.)

Chicano Starter Kit, 2008. Alicia Chavez and Jose Alvarez.
Photo by Sylvia Romo-Lara.

PROP 22
By Teatro Izcalli

CHARACTERS:

SPOT - Male in his fifties, wearing jeans, a t-shirt with an American flag on it, has a flash light, security badge on his chest.
KUJO - A dog puppet that's being held by Spot.
LUCY - Woman in her mid 50's. Wearing a wig.
LUPE - Good friend of Lucy around the same age. Wearing a wig as well.
JUAN - Dressed like a Mexican vaquero, wearing jeans, a cowboy hat, big belt buckle and gold chains around his neck.

Props: Small grill, four chairs, fake tortillas, and fake tacos.

(Spot *walks on stage.*)

SPOT: Hello my name is Roger Dodger, but you all can call me Spot. This here is my dog, Kujo, but you can call him Kujo.
KUJO: (*Starts barking, sound is made by* Spot.)

SPOT: You all know why I'm here right, right? You're right! I'm doing my
share to keep America to America for America by America. Why you
ask? Because they... they are coming by the millions and they're
sneaking in and taking our jobs! You all know who I'm talking
about... the illegals! They're taking our dreams right before our eyes
and I'm doing MY JOB to stop it! All right, all right. I may get a bit
emotional but I had dream.

KUJO: (*Starts whimpering.*)

SPOT: It's all right boy, it's all right. Yes, I had a dream of working as a dish
washer, getting paid minimum wage, with no health benefits,
and wearing fancy hairnets. I wanted to work with Ajax products to
the point it would affect my breathing, damage some brain cells,
perhaps even give me a little pneumonia, (Kujo *coughs.*) but the
illegals took that dream from me. (*Starts getting real emotional.*)
I had another dream to work in the fields in the hot sun for twelve
back breaking unbearable hours and be exposed to cancer causing
pesticides. (*He pauses and puts eye drops on his eyes.*) Yes, I was going to
pick lettuce and Kujo here was going to pick strawberries, his favorite
vegetable, but the illegals took that dream too.

KUJO: (Kujo *goes into* Spot's *pant pocket and pulls out a strawberry.*)

SPOT: So now I'm doing my job to keep America to America by America, so
America will feel like America. That's why I started my vigilant work
here at American theatres. I'm doing my duty to stop illegals from
sneaking in their mouth watering *chile con carne, tacos of ass-ada,
tamales, burritos, tostiloc*-nuts all that Mexican food into the local
movie theatres. Our motto here is snack bar or back to the car. That's
snack bar or back to the car.

KUJO: (*Quick bark.*)

SPOT: Why? I'll tell you why! Because if we don't stop them from sneaking
in those *tamales, carne con chile, quesadillas* we're in danger of losing
our thirty dollar all beef hotdogs or our three hundred calorie
pretzels. Ladies and gentlemen that's why I'm supporting Proposition
22, the Anti-*Chorizo Initiative.* Prop 22 will stop the illegals
from even bringing their food to the parking lots of movie theaters
or amusement parks. So ladies and gentlemen if you are not with us,
you are against us. Remember vote yes on Prop 22. Ladies and
gentlemen we're in danger of losing the American dream that's why
I say, snack bar or back to the car. (*Two* comadres *walk towards the
theatre. Chavo del Ocho music in the background.*)

LUCY: *Comadre.*

LUPE: *Digame comadre.*

LUCY: *Comadre.*

LUPE: *Gracias. Muchas gracias.*

el movimiento

101

LUCY: Hey *comadre* you're not trying to sneak food into the movies again? Right? I've been saving for six months so I can buy us some *nachos*.

LUPE: Are you crazy *comadre*? We're not spending thirty dollars on a soda. With thirty dollars I can get a tummy tuck in Tijuana.

LUCY: But *comadre*...remember the *perro*. We got kicked out last time. (*They approach* Spot.)

SPOT: Ladies, you know the policy. Snack bar or back to the car. You're not trying to sneak any outside food in this time, right?

LUCY: No, no, no...

LUPE: We have nothing.

SPOT: Don't try anything funny, ladies. (Kujo *barks as he sniffs their bags. He barks and scares them.*)

LUPE: (*Mumbling.*) *Perro cochino.*

SPOT: All right ladies you're good. I think Kujo says you're good. Go ahead. (*Comadres go take a seat in the theater. Quebradita music comes on.* Juan *enters dancing towards* Spot. *They both start dancing together.*)

SPOT: (*Stops dancing and starts screaming his lines.*) Snack bar or back to the car!

JUAN: No. No esnacks. *Nomas yo y mis botas. Y una* camera *pues para* make *un* bootleg *de* Estar Wars.

SPOT: Geesus *de Christo.* What is this? (*Grabs camera.*)

JUAN: It's a camera *para hacer* un bootleg *de* Estar Wars. (*Takes out a twenty dollar bill and hands it to* Spot. Spot *takes money then looks away.*)

SPOT: All right, all right. Hurry up. Get in.

JUAN: (Juan *goes off dancing to his seat. He sits behind the comadres. His phone rings.*) Hey *compa* let me call ju back. *Estoy en los* movies. Ju know Estar Wars? *Tiene un friego de Raza. ¿Como que quien? Pues Arturito, Chuy, Obi Juan Canobi y Hans Cholo.* Ok *pues, al rato.*

LUPE: Hey? (*Talking* to Juan.)

JUAN: Jes?

LUPE: Do you know *Chata*?

JUAN: *Chata*? No I don't know *Chata*.

LUPE: *Chata* the hell up!

JUAN: *Orale pues huerca.*

LUCY: *Comadre*, he called you a *puerca*!

LUPE: *Puerca tu abuela.*

LUCY: Hey *comadre*, I'm going to get some food. *Vengase, la invito.*

LUPE: No, no *comadre*. It's too expensive *y como esta la economia.* I have a little surprise. I hid it the other night. (*She reaches under her chair and pulls out a small grill with tacos cooking.*)

102

LUPE: *Tacos, comadre!*
LUCY: ¡*Ay comadre!* ¡*Que barbara!* Well … give me a *taco de asada.*
LUPE: Here it is with *salsa verde.*
SPOT: (*Runs in,* Kujo's *barking.*) Yes boy? Where's that smell coming from?
Is that *carne ass-ada?* Where did that come from! (*Pointing to the grill.*)
LUPE: I don't know. It was here.
SPOT: Are you sure?
LUPE: Yes. (*Looking innocently.*)
SPOT: (*Looks around.*) Give me *dos de ass-ada* (Kujo *barks.*) and three de buch for Kujo. (Kujo *barks again.*) And extra *guacamole* on the last three, I just love me some *tacos de ass-ada.* (*He exits the stage followed by* Lucy *and* Juan.)
LUPE: (*Stands up and moves center stage.*) Hi. Do you remember having to go the parking lot of Disneyland, the San Diego Zoo, and Sea World just so you and your family could enjoy some tortas and tacos? Or having to sneak in some rolled tacos into the movies? The reality is we just can't afford to pay fifteen dollars for a soda and nineteen dollars for nachos. That's why Comadres of California are working hard to put Proposition 22.5, the Family Food Act on this years' ballot. Prop 22.5 allows all Mexican moms to cook homemade food and bring it into any theme park, movie theatre, or tourist site in America. Yes, we will no longer have to think of creative ways to sneak food into the movies or amusement parks. I'm confident that united we can pass Prop 22.5 or the *Tengo un Chingo de Hambre* Act. Thank you.

(*End of* acto.)

Prop 22, 2009.
Michael Slomanson, Alicia Chavez, Claudia Cuevas.
Photo by Carlos Solorio.

Teatro Izcalli

Inspired by Youth

Teatro Izcalli

106

MARIABERTOS
By Macedonio Arteaga Jr. & Alicia Chavez

CHARACTERS:
MARIA - Has long braids, wearing a *huipil* Mexican dress and a sign that says "Maria".
CHUNKY - A heavy set man with a guitar, a very large mustache, and wearing a sign that says "Maria's Dad".
ANNOUNCER - Dressed in a suit and tie and wearing a sign that says "JUAN-800-555-TACO".
HOMEGIRL - Dressed as a chola and holding a can of Aquanet hair spray. Wearing a sign that says "Maria's Friend".

Props: Nothing is needed for the stage, just the props the characters have.

(Maria, Chunky, *and* Homegirl *are on stage with their backs to the audience.* Maria *is in the middle and each character turns to deliver their lines.*)

inspired by youth

MARIA: Hi my name is Maria. Thirteen years at San
    Diego State was taking too long and my minimum wage job was
    getting me nowhere.

So I decided to call ITT, the Institute of Taco Technology. Where I learned to make rolled tacos in 10 seconds flat and *chimichangas* faster than you can say *parangarancutirimicuaro*. And now I'm the proud owner of my own *taqueria*, Mariabertos.

HOMEGIRL: I'm Maria's friend, *¿y que?* You know before Maria went to ITT, home girl couldn't even flip a *tortilla* without using a spatulaaa. Now she even makes *mole* from scraaatch. I just want to say thank you Maria and thank you ITT 'cause now we have a Chicana owned establishment in the *barrio* with good food and at cheap priceeess. *Es todo. No, no es todo.* Hey Maria help me out. (Maria *holds up mirror and* Homegirl *sprays more hairspray onto hair.*) *Es todo.*

CHUNKY: I remember Maria. Yeah, I remember Maria because she's my daughter. That's how I remember Maria. I remember that day I was at the park and it was getting dark, and in the background you could hear a dog begin to bark. My daughter, my daughter Maria, comes to me and says (Maria *comes up to him and they say the following lines together.*)

MARIA AND CHUNKY: *Papasito, papasito pansón, ¿porque eres tan mamón? Te pareces mucho a un pedaso de jamón.*

CHUNKY: I remember that day like it was yesterday. My daughter Maria says to me, "*Papasito*, my future, it looks very blue, and I don't know what the hell do." So I say, "*Mijita, mijita* Maria, try ITT, the Institute of Taco Technology, and she did, and now my daughter Maria, she has a *taquería hasta la bahía.* (Chunky *starts playing the guitar.* Chunky *says lines simultaneously as* Maria *and* Homegirl *are singing.*)

CHUNKY: No *guacamole. ¿Con chile o sin chile?*

MARIA & HOMEGIRL: (*Singing.*) Mariabertos. Mariabertos. Not Gilbertos, not Albertos, not Robertos. Mariabertos. Mariabertos. Not Gilbertos, not Albertos, not Robertos. Mariabertos!

CHUNKY: No coke just Pepsi.

(*They all freeze.*)

ANNOUNCER: (*Walks in.*) Yes, you too can make your dreams come true like Maria. Call us at ITT THE INSTITUTE OF TACO TECHNOLOGY. All you need to do is pick up your phone and call JUAN-800-555-TACO. Yes, that's JUAN 800-555-TACO. Financial aid is available for those who qualify.

(*Everyone stomps their feet making a "tan tan" sound.*)

Teatro Izcalli   (*End of* acto.)

Mariabertos, 2008. Left: Claudia Cuevas, Mike Slomanson, and Hector Villegas. Photo by Sylvia Romo-Lara.

inspired by youth

Teatro Izcalli

Educación Mas Alta was written in collaboration with students that participated in Izcalli's 1997 Nahui Ollin Summer Project. Benny Madera and Victor Chavez Jr. were the two Teatro Izcalli members who facilitated the creation of this *acto* with the students. The *acto* was based on a true story by one of the female students whose father did not let her go away to college. Later contributors to the *acto* include Macedonio Arteaga Jr., Iyari Arteaga, Alicia Chavez, Claudia Cuevas, Ricky Medina, and Cristina Nuñez.

EDUCACIÓN MAS ALTA
By Teatro Izcalli

ARACTERS:
D - About fifty years old. Has a big belly and a mustache.
M - Wearing an apron.
KY - In 11th grade wearing big baggy clothes, shades and a beanie.
JA - A senior in high school, wearing a uniform.

ps: Fake butt, Ipod™, one chair.

ere's a chair with an Ipod™ on it in center stage.)
D: (*Enters the stage and walks around for a few seconds and then notices his daughter's Ipod™ on the chair, he walks over to pick it up.*) Oh my *mijas* left her mipa or something. You know they taught me in the hip *papí* classes that I should listen to my daughter's music so I can be hip also. I wonder how this *cochinada* works. How do you make this *cochinada* work? (*Trying to turn on Ipod™.*) Play. Play. (*Hip music starts playing.* Dad *turns his back to the audience and then he starts dancing slowly. Then he turns to audience dancing more "hip".*)

TINA: (*Walks in and yells.*) *Papí!* What are you doing with my Ipod™?

DAD: (*Reacting embarrassed and surprised. He presses down on the Ipod™ and it stops playing.*) Oh *mija* your mipa it was dirty and I was cleaning it with one of my *lonjas*. (*Changes the subject quickly.*) How was your day?

TINA: It was fine. Wow. Thanks for asking. You've never asked.

DAD: Well you know, *mija*, in those hip *papí* classes I've been going to, they told me to say, "how was your day?" to your children.

TINA: Okay well here's the mail, *papí*.

DAD: *Gracias, mija.* (*He reads the mail out loud.*) AT&T, cable, gas. Gas? Why do I have to pay for gas if I always have gas? *Hace poquito, mija,* I ripped one so loud that the house alarm went off.

TINA: *Papí,* that's gross. Plus we don't have a house alarm.

DAD: Esnap! Oh, it must have been the neighbor's. (*He struggles to read the following envelope.*) UUUSSSSCCC. USC. USC? *¿Que es eso, mija?*

TINA: USC, *papí.* The University of Southern California, it's a university.

DAD: Ooooohhhhh. Okay. (*Not really paying attention, looking at the other mail.*)

TINA: (*Opens the mail.*) Papí, I got accepted! I got accepted to go to USC! (Dad *and* Tina *jump around in a circle holding hands, saying lines simultaneously.*)

TINA: I got accepted! I got accepted! I got accepted!

DAD: You got accepted! You got accepted! You got accepted! (*Stops jumping.*) You got what?

TINA: Yes, *papí.* I got accepted to go to the university in Los Angeles, *papí.* Isn't that great?

DAD: (*Very upset.*) *Estás loca* if you think I'm going to let you go away to college in Los Angeles. *¿Pa que? ¿Para que andes de chile frito por alla? ¡Estás mensa!* Ju crazy!

TINA: But *papí,* what happened to those hip *papí* magazines you're reading?

DAD: Those hip *papí* magazines never talked about you going to Los Angeles. All it says is support your children's future decisions. That has nothing to do with you leaving the family.

TINA: *Papí,* can you hear yourself?

DAD: Of course, I can hear myself. And I can hear a little girl disrespecting her father.

TINA: *Aayyyy. ¡Amá! ¡Amá!* (Mom *comes in from the kitchen.*)

MOM: *¿Que está pasando?* What's going on here?

Teatro Izcalli Everyone calm down. *Todos están muy estresados.*

TINA: Mom, I got accepted to go to the university.

MOM: *Ay mija, que bueno* (*Hugs* Tina.)

TINA: But dad says that I can't go.

112

MOM: *¿Viejo, de que estás hablando?*

DAD: The only university you're going to is University Avenue down the street. Go get me some super nachos from Mariabertos.

RICKY: (*Enters stage.*) Whatzzzz up? (*Shakes hand with* Father *as they do a break dance move.*)

DAD: Whatz uppp!!!

MOM: I'll tell you whatz up, where have you been all day?

RICKY: (*Lying.*) I was…uh. . .at the library. Yeah.

DAD: (*Believing* Ricky *right away.*) Oh okay. . .

TINA: The library? You don't even know where the library is. You liar!

MOM: *¿Ah, sí?* At the library, eh. *Mentiroso.* They called me from your school and they told me you didn't go today.

RICKY: (*Scared.*) Yes, I did. I did. I was at the library all day.

MOM: *Viejo, dile algooo.*

DAD: (*Mimicking* Mom.) *Algooo.* (*He giggles a bit and* Mom *stares at him angrily.*) *Mijo,* if you want to go to college *tienes que ir a la escuela.*

TINA: College? How come he can go to college and I can't?

DAD: Well, for one thing, he's a boy. And you, *pues,* you're a girl.

TINA: *¿Y que?*

DAD: *¿Que de que? Mira, mija,* he's a boy, he has to support his family, and you will be supported by a man.

TINA: I don't need a man to take care of me. That's why I have a brain. (Tina *and* Mom *snap their fingers in Z formation.*)

DAD: (*Looking at* Mom.) *¿Que es esto de esnap, esnap, esnap! ¡¿Que hijos de las papas le estas enseñando a esta niña?!*

MOM: She didn't learn it from me, probably MTV three. Everybody shut up sus *bocás* please! We'll talk about this later. Ricky, (Mom *snaps fingers.*) assume the position in the corner. (Ricky *gets on his knees with both arms stretched out.*)

RICKY: But, but, ma…

MOM: Stay in the position. (*Walks over to* Dad, *who's sitting on a chair.*) *Viejo,* (*Massaging his shoulders.*) remember when we went to Tijuana for our honeymoon and we ate all of those *tacos.* Remember how those *tacos de adobada* did you so wrong that you couldn't even perform. (Dad *crosses his legs and gives a small cry of shock.*) It's okay, *viejo.* It happens to everyone. Anyway, *viejo,* do you remember how we talked about the future and dreams we had for our children … about going to college? Well, now our daughter's dream is coming true. She has a chance to go to a great university…

DAD: You're absolutely right, *vieja.* (*All of the sudden, he snaps and starts yelling.*) *¡No y no!* (*Stands up.*) She's not going! No daughter of mine is going away to college!

113

MOM: (*Turns to* Dad *sweetly.*) *Viejo, vete a comer. Ya está la comida. Andale.* (Dad *walks off to the kitchen angry.*)

TINA: Mom, I really want to go to college.

MOM: *Aver, dame los papeles, mija.* I'll sign them. You're going to college. *No sé como le vamos hacer* but you're going to college.

TINA: But I need papí's signature too.

MOM: *Ay, mija,* your dad doesn't even know how to read. Who do you think signs all of the checks around here?

TINA: What about those *Hip Papí Magazines* he reads?

MOM: *Ay, mija,* you're so innocent sometimes, he just looks at the pictures.

TINA: *Gracias, mamí.* (*They hug. Then* Tina *walks off to the kitchen.*)

MOM: (*Turns to* Ricky.) *¡Y tu! Más vale que no te la vayas a pintiar otra ves.* Clean up this *sala. Luego te vas a comer.*

RICKY: Aw, mom.

MOM: *Mijo,* do you really think you're fooling me? You may be fooling your father but it's not going to work on me. What are you going to do with your life? You want to work hard like your father? Look, *mijo,* let me show you something that I thought I would never have to share with you. (*She brings out a fake butt from the closet.*) See this, *mijo.* What does this look like?

RICKY: That's gross. It looks like someone's *nalgas,* someone's butt.

MOM: Well, *mijo,* you're right. These are your father's *nalgas.* He's worked so hard *mijo,* that he worked his butt off. Your father has no more *nalgas.* When I want to grab his butt, I have to go to the closet to grab them. (*She's nearly in tears.*) Is this what you want? *¡Miralas!*

RICKY: Okay, mom. Could you please put dad's *nalgas* away? That's really gross. (Mom *puts the* nalgas *away.*) I promise I'll start trying but mom, it's hard to really study. First, you and dad can never help me with my homework and we don't even have a computer.

MOM: Look, *mijo,* we're not like other families. I know we haven't helped you much. Heck, *mijo,* the closest thing we have to a computer is a calculator that's missing the 0 and 5. But I'll talk to your *tio* about getting us a used computer.

RICKY: The one that hooked up cable illegally for us?

MOM: Shush, *mijo,* your dad doesn't know that your *tio* did that. Look, your sister is going to college and you can too. What do you want to do when you grow up?

Teatro Izcalli

RICKY: I would like to be a writer, mom. I've decided I'm going to try harder.

MOM: That's great, *mijo.* You would be a great writer. Let's tell your father and sister. *¡Viejo! ¡Mija!* (Tina *and* Dad *return.*) *Viejo,* I want to continue talking about our daughter and also our son.

DAD: I know, *vieja*. Listen, family. All this stuff is hard for me. The classes I'm taking are helping me slowly. Don't expect me to change over night but I'm learning. I'm learning to express my emotionals. I've thought about it, and *mija*, it hurts my heart, (*He's pounding on his heart.*) but if you want to go to college, I'll let you go.

TINA: *Papí*, you're the best. (*Goes and hugs Dad.*)

MOM: *Viejo*, I knew it. I love you so much my little *torta de jamón*.

DAD: *Ayyy, vieja*, stop it. Please not in front of the children.

MOM: Well, our little Ricky also has news. Tell them Ricky.

RICKY: Well, I promise I'll start doing better in school. And I want to go to college and be a writer.

DAD: (*Raising his voice a bit.*) A writer? Why not a doctor or a lawyer? What in the world do writers do anyway?

MOM: *Viejo*. (*Trying to calm him down.*)

TINA: *Papí*, they write. They can write plays, movies, for newspapers, magazines and sitcoms. They can write books...

DAD: Okay, okay. This has been a bit too much for me. I feel a bit nervous about all these changes coming up.

RICKY: Oh no.

TINA: What?

MOM: You know what happens when your dad gets nervous, *mija*. ¡Las nalgas! (*They all run out and you hear a big fart.*)

DAD: I really miss my butt. Where can it be? (*He whistles for his butt, like you would call a dog.*) Come here *nalgas*. Come here.

(*End of* acto.)

ABUELITA
By Macedonio Arteaga Jr.

CHARACTERS:

ABUELITA - A man dressed as an old lady wearing a dress with a cane.
CHAVA - A baby played by an adult male wearing a giant diaper and no shirt.
CHITA - A little girl with pig tails around seven years old.
QUETZAL - Little girl eight years old.

(Quetzal *and* Chita *fighting on stage over a doll.*)
CHITA: (*Pulling on a doll that* Quetzal *is holding on to.*) That's my doll.
QUETZAL: No, that's my doll. *Tio* Pepe gave it to me on my birthday.
CHITA: No he gave it to me because I'm his favorite. You're a *fuchi* face.
QUETZAL: No you're *fuchi*. (Quetzal *pulls the doll away and* Chita *falls on the floor and starts crying.*)
CHITA: ¡*Abuelita*! ¡*Abuelita*! (Abuelita *walks on stage. Native American flute music plays in the background. She comes in holding* Chava's *hand.*)

Teatro Izcalli

ABUELITA: Shut up your mouthies *mijas*. You woke up the baby. Sit down
   mijo. Sit down. (Chava *lets go of* Abuelita *and falls to the ground.*
   Abuelita *walks closer to the audience.*) What are you laughing about?
   Because my chichis are falling? Well you're a lot younger than me
   and your *chichis* are falling. When I was your age I had back and I
   looked good, *chiquilla mocosa.* (Chava *is still crying.*) *Mijo*, shut
   up your *boca.* (*Takes out a giant baby bottle from under her sweater.*)
   Here *mijo*. Okay *mijos*, I want to tell you a story. You guys want to
   hear a story?
CHITA: Yes, *abuelita.* Tell us a story about the *rancho.*
ABUELITA: Sush, sush. I want to tell you a story about (*She pauses.*) the
   devil.
CHITA & QUETZAL: (*Screaming scared.*) Aaaahhh! No!
ABUELITA: Yes *mijas.* This is something that happened to me when I was
   very young.
QUETZAL: Wow that must have been a long, long, long time ago.
ABUELITA: (*Taps* Quetzal *with the cane.*) Shush *mocosa*. Shush. A long
   time ago we used to be very, very poor. We were so poor the only
   thing we had to eat was rocks with two beans. Yes two beans and
   rocks. We would suck on the rocks that were in the pot with the
   beans. One day me and your *Tio Cuauhtémoc* had to walk to
   go get milk from another ranch, but we had to walk like thirty
   thousand kilometers and we had to cross a river.
CHITA: Like the *Rio Grande?*
ABUELITA: Yes, but three thousand twenty two point five kilometers longer,
   mijita.
CHITA: Wow, must have been hard on the *huaraches.*
ABUELITA: (*Gives her a harsh look.*) Don't get funny *mija*. I'm telling a
   story. Yes, me and your *tio* started to cross the river and we held
   on tightly so we would not fall and get swallowed by the river. As
   we were crossing the river something began to happen. The wind all
   of the sudden began to get stronger (*Wind plays in the background.*)
   and stronger. The sun hid behind the clouds and darkness took over
   the land. We both started to get very scared, for we knew something
   was out there.
QUETZAL: (*Very scared.*) What was it *abuelita?* What was it?
ABUELITA: *Mija* we began to hear a noise. A terrible noise. (*You hear a loud
   scary noise like a monster. Both girls scream and* Chava *is now real
   close to the* Abuelita.) In the middle of the
   river was a big rock. We knew the noise was
   coming from there, but we didn't want to look
   back. We could hear a monster jumping on the rock. We were almost
   across the river when we looked over and saw him. IT WAS THE

inspired by youth

117

DEVIL!! Yes, *mijas* he had a chicken leg and the other leg of a *chivo*. Yes, a goat. When I looked at him, fire came out of his mouth like this (*She opens her mouth making a funny noise like fire is coming out of her mouth.*) and he had two little horns on his head. Yes he did. Me and your *tio* ran and ran and never looked back. Later we heard in the village that a stranger had showed up wearing nice clothes and ended up taking several women from the village. He left a terrible odor in the village that did not go away for sixty-two years, *mijas*. Yes it was the devil. *Esta bien cochino nunca se baña el marrano.* (*She starts sniffing around and walks closer to audience.*) I smell *cacarocha*. (*She walks closer to the girls and then to* Chava.) Aagghh *cochino!* You did *cacarocha*. Come on lets go get you changed. (*She exitswith* Chava.)

QUETZAL: Chava did *cacarocha*. (Chita *and* Quetzal *skip off stage singing.*) *Cacarocha...*

(*End of* acto.)

I was visiting a school to meet with an elementary school counselor when I saw a boy about ten year's old waiting to see a counselor. His hands were shaking and he was even pulling his hair. He was holding a piece of paper with him and I was going to ask him why he was in the office when the counselor came out to greet me. Why is this boy here I asked. He's here because he was drawing obscenities in class. I asked if I could see what he had drawn. The counselor handed me the paper and it took me about a second to know what it was. I was so angry. This is what the little boy had drawn:

He had drawn a piñata, breaking. I was so upset from this incident. However, later it inspired me to write and perform the following *acto*. Piñata was performed as improv on stage and was written down many years later.

PIÑATA DAD
By Macedonio Arteaga Jr.

CHARACTERS:

CHACHO - Dad in his fifties has a heavy Chicano accent and sounds like an old homeboy from the *barrio*. Dressed nice with a zoot suit and wearing a hat and shades. Also does the voice of Obi Wan Kenobi from Star Wars.
SON - Six years old, looks dorky and is uncoordinated.
TREE - A person holding a small tree branch. Stands there holding the *piñata*, can be a volunteer from the audience.
KIDS - Three or four people, can be volunteers from the audience.
LITTLE GIRL - Ten years old, wearing a Jedi cloak as seen in Star Wars.

(*Scene starts with* Chacho *walking on stage to swing music.*)
CHACHO: (*He snaps his fingers and the music stops.*) Orale. ¿Que honda. ¿Que les pasa? Se parecen mucho a una calabasa. My name is Chacho and I'm here to tell you a story. I'm here to revive a moment in life. It's a story that goes back in time, back to Roman times, to *Mexica* times, to *Toltec* times. It goes so far back in time I forgot what time. It's a

story about a man, a man becoming a man, a man growing up to be a man, being confused about being a man. Oh no that's a different story. It's a story of a man and his son, the saga of all sagas. Our family had been cursed for hundreds of years, we weren't able to break a *piñata* or even get a candy for centuries. So the day my *chavalito* was born I began to prepare to break the curse. Yeah man, I remember I had trained my *chavalito* for this day for many years. Even when he was in his cradle he had a little stick, preparing for the big day. He was preparing to break his first *piñata*. (Son *comes out on stage and falls immediately*.) Oh yeah, we had worked out real hard. Remember, *mijo*? (Son *is oblivious to what* Chacho *is saying*.) We did Tae bo™, you know everybody knows all of those videos to get my *chavalito* in shape. Boy, he was intense. I remember our intense, immense jogging days. (*They start jogging in place*.)

SON: *Papí*, why does that lady have a mustache?

CHACHO: *Mijo*, stop staring. It's not good to stare. Plus you're one hundred percent focused on breaking the *piñata*. Remember, *mijo*. (Chacho *looks over*.) Dang, she does have a mustache. (*Looks back at* Son.) Oh, *mijo*, are you listening to me? We need to be ready for when the big day comes.

SON: Yes, *papí*.

CHACHO: Finally at age six, they invited my son to a birthday party. Yeah, he was going to get a shot at breaking his first *piñata*. I remember getting the invitation. Chacho we're having a *piñata* party at our house, hurry up, the party already started and bring some *nachos*. (Tree *walks on stage with a* piñata.) We got to the party and the big moment was set. The children were ready (Kids *run on stage*.) *Orale*, a tree that can move. Okay, I remember as my *chavalito* was preparing for the first big moment of his life. They put a bandanna over his eyes, spun him around a few times, and they began to sing the *piñata* song. (*Audience sings along*.) I knew he was visualizing what I had taught him. I could see him breaking the *piñata* and the old curse. He was about to swing, when all of a sudden the *morro* started throwing up all over himself. (Son *starts throwing up*.) That's okay, *mijo*. That's okay. I quickly began cleaning up. (Chacho *starts doing a river dance move, stomping away the vomit on the floor*.) *Orale*. (*Does pachuco stance*.)

SON: *Orale*. (*Does pachuco stance as well*.)

CHACHO: Yeah, we cleaned it all up and everyone
agreed to give my son another chance. You guys better give my *mijo* another chance or we're gonna have problems and you all know I don't like to have problems. I could feel it in the air like dirty underwear. I knew he could do it. He

was ready. There was my son. He flexed his muscles and took a swing so powerful—boom! You could hear the mighty blow, (*Makes a loud noise with microphone. Son strikes himself on the head.*) but he had hit his big *cabeza* ¡*Chale*, the *morro*...well, he knocked himself out. (*Son falls to the ground.*) People were saying, "Hey, Chacho, is that your son?" Na, man, *chale* I don't know who that little *mocoso* is. My son's at home working on the theory of reverse osmosis. (*Walks over to* Son.) *Mijo*, get up, *mijo*. It's just a little hit. It's okay, *mijo*. It's okay.

SON: (*He gets up and looks dazed.*) *Y los candies? Y los candies?*

CHACHO: No *mijo*, the candies haven't come out yet. Well, you know what, *mijo*? If you couldn't break it, that's all right. You can get all the candy when they break the *piñata*. Remember how I taught you. When they break the *piñata*, you dive in like a hawk. Remember how I taught you? (*Chacho acts like he's a hawk.* Son *nods his head but looks awkward.*) It was finally another little girl's turn. Listen *mijo*, you can still break the curse. Yeah by just getting candies you can break half the curse. (*The* Kids *split in half and a* Little Girl *walks up through the middle. She raises her hand and* Chacho *tosses her the* piñata *stick, as if it flew off his hand.*) After that, I heard some crazy voice coming out of the *pinche* tree or something. It was talking to the little girl. (*Speaks in* Voice of Obi Wan Kenobi.) Use the force *morrita*. Use the force. (*Chacho speaks in regular voice.*) Then the little girl put the hood over her head. She looked like a little Chicana Jedi. She put her hand out and all of a sudden the *piñata* started shaking. (*Tree shakes the* piñata.) Then the tree started shaking. Then boom, the *piñata* fell to the ground sending candies all over the place. (*All the* Kids *jump in and start grabbing candies.*) After the candies fell to the ground my son dove in like a hawk swooping up the candy, like if there was no *mañana*. (*Walks over to* Son, *who's standing there not moving.*) *Metete baboso.* (*Kicks him in the butt.* Son *falls to the ground face down and lay's there.*) Well, it didn't work out for him. The children were picking up his *lonja* and grabbing candies. They even started taking his shoes and socks. (Kids *take his shoes, socks and hat.*) *Mijo*, are you all right, *mijo*? (*The* Kids *run off stage.*)

SON: Sí, *papi. Mira* candy. (*He's holding something brown in his hand.*)

CHACHO: You did it, *mijo*. You got some candy! I think you broke the curse of the nurse. (*He grabs the candy from his* Son's *hand.*) No *mijo*, that's not candy! It's *caca* from the poodle next door. (*He drops the* caca.) *Sacate mocoso! Cochino.* (Son *runs out crying.*) After that evening when we went home, I finally made the call. You know, the call. I called the *Piñata* Rehab Center.

There I learned about the most important things in life. Yes, they helped me to understand that spending quality time with your kids is the most important thing in the world. Helping them to read and write. It doesn't matter how many *piñatas* your *morritos* break. No way, homes, it's all about quality time. Their *mota*, I mean, their motto is if anyone can, a Mexi-Can. I still remember that. Thank you once more *Piñata* Rehab Center. *Orale.*

(*End of* acto.)

ESCUELITA
By Teatro Izcalli

CHARACTERS:

TEACHER - Mr. Henry is middle-aged. He's been drinking because his wife left him.

CUAUHTÉMOC - Male, high school student wearing a t-shirt with the Aztec calendar and a bandana on his head.

DUDE - Skater who comes on stage riding a skateboard, wearing a helmet.

BRAIN - Has large glasses and has his/her pants pulled up very high.

TRACY - Is blond and wearing a cheerleading outfit.

(*Scene starts as students walk in and sit down.* Tracy *is last to enter. She takes a slice of pizza out of her backpack and places it on the teacher's desk. The* Teacher *is not on stage yet. School bell rings.* Cuauhtemoc *walks to the teacher's desk and takes out a stun gun. He removes the batteries.*)

TRACY: (*Sits next to* Brain.) Oh what cute shoes and
I love your hair. Like I think your glasses are so adorable. Okay I know we're really not friends and I'll probably never be your friend,

but I have to talk to someone about this it's like eating me up. Like these last two weeks have been the most challenging of my life. Like did you hear they kicked me off the cheer leading team? Of course you heard like everyone is talking about it. I really don't care about cheer even though I was the best flyer and anyway they're going to suck without me. Anyway I can do other things like playing gymnast or learn tennis. I'm really good at catching like my mom says. It's not like I don't have a life besides cheer. Like this school is crazy just because I turned in a paper that wasn't mine they shouldn't have kicked me off cheer for that. They said it was plager erasing. Like nobody even knows what that means. Like, I didn't even erase anything. And what does plager erasing have to do with cheer I just don't see the connection. Who cares anyway, it's just cheer, right? (*She gets sad and starts crying.*) Oh my god, I miss cheer. I really miss cheer so much. I can't live without cheer.

BRAIN: I would highly recommend psychological treatment, classmate.

CUAUHTÉMOC: Dang home girl, you're on a good one, *loca.*

TRACY: Whatever.

TEACHER: (*Enters speaking loudly.*) Good morning class.

ALL STUDENTS: (*Except* Tracy.) Good morning, Mr. Henry.

TRACY: Um Mr. Hungry, I brought you a slice of pizza, its like, on your desk.

TEACHER: Thank you, Tracy and I'm Mr. Henry not Hungry. So let's get started on today's lesson. We'll have the honor and the privilege to learn about one of the greatest men of all time, Christopher Columbus. Just because my wife left me, it doesn't mean he wasn't a brave man. He was a great man, who was brave enough to discover America. She said she needed to find herself. Maybe if she would have sailed with Columbus, she would have discovered herself. (*Puts his head down on the desk then looks up.*) Yes, I'm listening, class. I'm listening. She said I never listened. I always listened. (*Cries a bit.*) Alright, alright, yes, yes. Now back to Columbus. (Tracy *raises her hand.*) Yes, Tracy?

TRACY: Did you all know, like, because of Columbus we now have like the Columbus Day Special, where you get like, great bargains at all the malls. I got these cute shoes and matching purse on the last Columbus Day Special. Aren't they just adorable?

DUDE: Yeah, I even got my skateboard half off at the "Columbus Goes Skateboarding Day" at Big 5. We need to be thankful for that dude discovering America.

CUAUHTÉMOC: Columbus? That fool was lost. He didn't discover anything.

TEACHER: Do we have a problem young man? As a matter of fact, I do have

124

a problem, I have been lost ever since she left me. If only Columbus could help me find a new world, a new beginning.

CUAUHTÉMOC: I'm tired of hearing that lie about Columbus discovering America. History on this continent does not start with Columbus. I wasn't discovered and my ancestors weren't discovered. We had advanced civilizations here, way before that *vato* got lost.

TRACY: Oh, no. Mr. Hungry, I'm like getting scared.

TEACHER: Now, now, (*Looking at* Cuauhtémoc.) Nowwww… what was your name again?

CUAUHTÉMOC: Cuauhtémoc Sanchez.

TEACHER: Cua, Cuak, Kool Aid, what? That's too difficult to pronounce. From now on, we'll just call you, ummhh… Tim. Tim lets try not to intimidate other students consider this is your first warning.

CUAUHTÉMOC: Tim? My name is Cuauhtémoc, not Tim!

TEACHER: Now listen, Tim. This is not a good way to start off the semester. You may be entitled to your opinion, but it doesn't mean you have to bully the class. Now as I was saying, in fourteen hundred and ninety-two, my wife left me, like Columbus left Spain. She sailed the…sailed the ocean blue…

CUAUHTÉMOC: We've learned about Columbus since we were in first grade and we don't even learn the truth. Did you know that Columbus used to cut the Taino's ears and noses if they didn't give him enough gold. He was no hero. So why can't we learn about a modern hero, a real hero, like César Chávez. Why can't we learn Chicano history?

TEACHER: Tim, Tim, Tim. I warned you. (*Pulls out a stun gun, points it at* Cuauhtémoc *and stuns him once.* Cuauhtémoc, *shakes in his seat.*) Wow! This works great! (*Students are shocked.*) He'll be fine class. Instead of giving students referrals or suspensions we have been issued stun guns.

DUDE: Wow. Can I get zapped like that? It looks pretty cool.

TEACHER: If I zapped you Dude, your parents would sue me. That's the last thing I need, another person suing me. She wants everything, understand? Even the little goldfish. (*He makes a goldfish face and acts like he's swimming.*) Get the picture? ¿Comprendes?

DUDE: Yeah, dude, I get the picture. You're hurting. *No problema. Hasta la vista, mis amigos. Yo quiero carne asada* fries.

BRAIN: Mr. Henry, I really liked what Cuauhtémoc had to say I would highly encourage that dialogue if possible.

TEACHER: Okay Brain, since you asked so nicely. inspired by youth Alright, Hispanic history…César Chávez… fine, I'll quickly discuss Cesar the Great. He was a great boxer who rarely lost a fight.

125

CUAUHTÉMOC: (*Still shaking in his seat.*) What?

TEACHER: Everyone calm down I'm fine.

BRAIN: Uh Mr. Henry, Cuauhtémoc was referring to César Chávez, not Julio César Chávez the boxer. You know, César Chávez, the great Chicano farm labor leader and humanitarian. He was the founder of the United Farm Workers Union who fought for union wages, equal housing, and social justice for farm workers.

DUDE: Dude, I didn't know Columbus was all crazy like that. And yeah, we need to learn more about Cesar and how he organized the farm workers. Dude, they pick our *carne asada* we should help them out.

CUAUHTÉMOC: Dude, farm workers don't pick *carne asada* it comes from a cow *vato loco*.

TEACHER: Didn't I tell you to be quiet, Tim?

CUAUHTÉMOC: But, but ...

TEACHER: Tim, stop with the butt I have no butt to go home to anymore. (*He cries a bit more.* Cuauhtémoc *looks confused and walks over to console* Teacher. Teacher *stuns him and everyone looks at* Cuauhtémoc *as he falls to the floor.*) He'll be fine. Alright, alright lets all settle down now. I had settled down. I was willing to do anything she wanted but nooooo... she said she had to grow. So with that in mind I will continue with Brain's suggestion. I will lead a discussion on Hispanic history.

CUAUHTÉMOC: (Cuauhtémoc *struggles to get up.*) Chicano history, teacher. (Teacher *stuns him again.*)

TEACHER: Yes, yes. Okay, is it necessary to have Chicano history in schools? That is the question.

TRACY: First of all Mr. Hungry. I don't really understand why like we should have Chico-ano history. I don't mean to be rude but why do we have to learn about foreigners? Like, we where here first. Like, I want to learn white history before we're forced to learn about them. Like, all we learn about is like George Washington and Abraham Lincoln and Dave the Crocket, but not about white history.

BRAIN: Mr. Henry, fellow classmates, first of all we learn about white history everyday. Now on the other hand, our country has neglected the education of Chicano history to millions of students. Also, Chicanos are not foreigners. Chicanos have been on this land way before the arrival of the Europeans and are descendents of many indigenous tribes from here in the United States and from Mexico. Teaching Chicano history should be the norm not something that needs to be fought for.

Teatro Izcalli

DUDE: (*Gets closer to* Brain.) You rock girl.

TRACY and BRAIN: (*Together.*) Creepy.

TEACHER: (*Puts zapper away.*) Well...uh... I...uh...you're right.

CUAUHTÉMOC: (*Stands up.*) Mr. Henry, the stun gun wasn't working. I took the batteries out of that thing before you walked in. (*He's holding the batteries in his hand.*)

TEACHER: You did what?

CUAUHTÉMOC: Come on man, it's time for you to get with the program, Mr. Henry. I want everyone to learn about the great accomplishments of César Chávez and the struggle of Chicano's. Mr. Henry, I also think you need to get some counseling, *estas pirata.*

BRAIN: I concur with that.

DUDE: Yea, dude.

TRACY: Find some batteries and zap him again. He's so like against Ameri cans. Look what he started?

DUDE: Hey Tracy, I think behind that fear of not being accepted by others you're a rocking chick.

TRACY: Dude, (*She pauses.*) I have to admit I have like always been afraid of people of the color and, and (*Crying.*) I just miss cheer. I miss it so much. (*She puts her head down.*)

CUAUHTÉMOC: Hey Dude, *estas pesado.* That was deep *vato.*

TEACHER: Tracy, are you going to be okay?

TRACY: (*Raises her head.*) Yes like I think so.

BRAIN: Wow, Dude. Where did you get that insight from?

DUDE: Well dude partially from Master Yoda, but when given the opportunity and the right environmental setting, my mom says I can be brilliant.

BRAIN: Well, Dude, that was brilliant.

DUDE: Yeah? You liked it? Well, would you like to join me for an iced *moco* later?

BRAIN: Dude, I think you mean an iced mocha. Iced *moco* means iced booger in Spanish.

DUDE: Yeah, that's what I meant, dude, iced mocha.

BRAIN: Well, as long as it's not Starbucks. I boycott that place.

DUDE: You're my kind of woman, power to the people! ¡*Viva César Chávez,* dude!

TEACHER: Alright, Romeo and Juliet. I may be a bit depressed but I can see how important this is. (*His phone rings.*) Hello, yes, yes my buttercup. Yes, I'll do what it takes. Yes, yes we'll make it work. I'm in class. Let me call you back. Class, she's going to give me another chance!

TRACY: Um, wait Mr. Henry, I want to tell the class I learned a lot today. Tim, I don't want to be afraid of you any more. But if I'm not taught about your foreign culture, how am I supposed to understand your people?

CUAUHTÉMOC: You're alright home girl. You're alright and you make a good point. I would like to take you to Chicano Park one day so you can learn more about our struggle. (Tracy *looks very scared.*) Don't trip home girl, you'll be fine.

TRACY: Can I like do a cheer at the park?

CUAUHTÉMOC: *Orale, porque no?*

TEACHER: (*Very happy*) We can make it a class field trip. We'll discuss it next week. She's going to give me a second chance!

(*End of* acto.)

Teatro Izcalli

Commissioned Works

Teatro Izcalli

130

The following works are all commissioned pieces. For one of the projects, we were hired by the San Diego Commission for Arts and Culture and taught theatre in all of the San Ysidro elementary schools for three years (2001-2004). We collaborated with Victor Ochoa, who taught visual art, and Miguel-Angel Soria from the Taco Shop Poets, who taught poetry. Teatro Izcalli helped the students write short *actos* and produce their work. The collaboration resulted in two published books and a video, all of which were given to the participants and the community. Other commissioned projects include a teen pregnancy prevention video, promoting the Census (2000), and a theatrical production and video geared to parents with children 0 to 5 years old.

Front cover of student book.
Artwork by Victor Ochoa.

Teatro Izcalli

I was working with a teen pregnancy prevention program in San Diego when I watched a teen pregnancy prevention video by an African–American comedian. After viewing the video, I thought of writing something like that for Chicano students. Teatro Izcalli then received a grant from the California Arts Council in 2002 and we produced this *acto* as a video with students from Mission Bay High School. We had nearly thirty Chicano students involved with the production of this video along with Albert Rascon who directed. The most important aspect of this production was that we showed the school that Chicano students did want to get involved in something other than soccer and gang banging. I say this because many times you hear school staff where Chicano students get bused into, that the Latino kids don't want to get involved in anything. I've used this video when I do teacher trainings to demonstrate the importance of CULTURALLY RELEVENT INSTRUCTIONAL STRATEGIES.

PREVENTION MENTIONED ¿Y QUE?
By Macedonio Arteaga Jr.

CHARACTERS:

SANCHO - A teenage boy.
HILDRINA - A teenage girl.
SINGER - Sings Marvin Gaye song "Lets get it on".
PACHUCO - Dressed in a zoot suit, sounds like the *pachuco* played by Edward James Olmos in the play Zoot Suit.
SEXUALLY TRANSMITTED DISEASES (Gonorrhea, herpes, syphilis, HIV/AIDS) - Dressed in monster outfits with signs on their chest, that spell their names.
WRESTLER - Dressed as a Mexican wrestler with a mask.
MILITARY MAN - Dressed in camouflage and face painted military style.
PIMP - Wearing gold chains, shirt unbuttoned, and slick hair.
CHOLO - Wearing dark shades and a buttoned up flannel.
HIPPIE - Dressed like a hippie.
TARZAN - Dressed like Tarzan.
BLONDE GIRL - Talks like a valley girl.

commissioned works

133

PUERTO RICAN GIRL - Has a shirt with the Puerto Rican flag on it.

CHOLA – Dressed like a *chola* and wearing dark shades.

REVOLUTIONARY - Woman dressed like an *Adelita* from the Mexican Revolution.

(Sancho *and* Hildrina *are sitting on a couch.*)

SANCHO: Hildrina, baby, your big beautiful eyes remind me of the cows I used to herd in my *pueblo* of *Tlahuwanipa*.

HILDRINA: Stop it, Sancho. You're making me melt, like the cheese on a warm *quesadilla*.

SANCHO: You know, I love you Hildrina, we've been together for one week now. I think it's time we show our love.

HILDRINA: Don't you think it's too soon?

SANCHO: Of course not! Hildrina, you're the love of my life for this week. I just feel we already have bonded my beautiful hot *enchilada de queso*.

HILDRINA: Oh Sancho, your words make me so hungry for your love, but bonded? How have we bonded? Do you really think we have bonded?

SANCHO: Well, yes, remember how we both got scared by Kujo my neighbor's dog? Remember how I ran and you ran behind me because I was so scared?

HILDRINA: Oh, yes, that was so romantic, Sancho. Gosh, Sancho, you really got me thinking. You're just so good with words. You remind of Picasso, the French poet.

SANCHO: Wasn't Picasso a painter?

HILDRINA: Maybe, but I just want to use the French language because they say French is the language of love.

SANCHO: You're right. Wow, talk to me in French some more.

HILDRINA: Picasso, french fries, french dip, french toast, *si vous plis*, french kissing.

SANCHO: Oh my Hildrina, speak no more! You're making my blood boil. (*He stands up and talks straight to the audience.*) Holy *posole*! It sounds like it's on like donkey kong but there's one problem. All this French talk has got me so excited. I'm pretty sure we're going to get BUSY WITH IT! (*He does a little dance.*) But I don't have a condom. Well, what should I do? (a) Tell her to stop and wait while I go get a condom, (b) completely lie to her and tell her I have never had sex with anyone but myself. (c) Lie, lie, lie, lie, and get it on. Who needs a condom anyway? (d) Not have sexual intercourse

tonight. (*He pauses to think.*) I think I will go with C. Well, Hildrina, I have a surprise for you. (*He claps his hands and the lights dim.* Singer *appears singing "Lets get it on".*)

SANCHO: I told you to sing from the closet, fool.

134

SINGER: I'm sorry, man. I never get it right.

SANCHO: All right, fool, get going. I got business to handle. (*Singer exits.*)

HILDRINA: Wow, Sancho, you're the bomb! You're making me feel special. Well, do you have protection?

SANCHO: Oh yes, baby, you know I'm always prepared for you, Hildrina. (*Reaches over and grabs a mouthpiece and a football helmet and puts them both on.*)

HILDRINA: Are you sure that's all the protection we need?

SANCHO: Of course, Hildrina. You're my first. I've never been with anyone else. Plus you're more precious than the rays of the sun. (*He winks at the audience and they look at each other. They're about to hug when* Pachuco *appears in the room out of no where.*)

PACHUCO: Orale, *calmontes montes. Patas chicas. ¿Que onda? Con esto molesto.*

SANCHO: (*Stands up.*) Hey, how did you get in here? (*He does some karate and boxing moves, then charges after* Pachuco *head down with his football helmet.*)

PACHUCO: (*Puts his hand out and holds* Sancho *back, then throws him back on the couch.*) *No seas mamón, jamón. Trucha con la carrucha.* What do you both think you're doing? Making love without a glove helps none of the above. ¡*Orale*!

SANCHO: But we thought this was all the protection we needed.

PACHUCO: No way, *vato.* You need real protection after you get an erection. You need to wear a condom. (*Pulls out a condom and snaps it at* Sancho.) *No seas mensorón.*

SANCHO: A condom? No way. Those are very uncomfortable. Plus they make those things too small. (*He flexes.*)

PACHUCO: *Calmontes*, King Kong. First of all, you're smaller than my pinky, winky. (*He puts up his pinky and winks.* Sancho *covers himself. Meanwhile,* Pachuco *has his hand all the way in the condom.*) If you can't fit into this, then you need to be making your flicks with some *loca* chicks. No offense to women, but that's the only word that rhymes with flicks. *Orale.*

HILDRINA: But, Mr. Pachuco, I haven't slept around. (*She does the sign of the cross.*)

SANCHO: Yeah, she hasn't slept around, so what's the problem?

PACHUCO: Oh yeah. She hasn't slept alone in her *cantón.* That's all that has been known. (*He snaps his fingers.*) ¡¡*Orale*!! (*Six men show up behind her. One is a* Wrestler, *a Military Man, a* Cholo, *a* Pimp, *a Hippie, and* Tarzan.)

commissioned works

ALL MEN TOGHETHER: HILDRINA!!! (*One by one, they take center stage. Wrestler flexes in front of the audience and makes a grunting noise, then exits.*)

135

MILITARY MAN: I'll go to war for you, Hildrina. (*Exits.*)

HILDRINA: I've never seen him in my life.

CHOLO: *¿Que onda*, shy girl? I guess you're not that shy after all? (*Exits.*)

PIMP: (*Just looks ahead counting all of his money and exits the stage.*)

HIPPIE: I thought we were spiritually connected, Hildrina. (*Exits.*)

TARZAN: Me Tarzan, you Hildrina. (*Exits.*)

PACHUCO: Having sex at such a young age is a complete rage, so did you use protection for the infection? Not only is Sancho sleeping with all the men you slept with but he's also sleeping with all the women that your partners slept with. It's a vicious cycle that goes on and on and on and on. *¿Me entiendes, Mendez?*

HILDRINA: Yes, yes, I understand, but what about him? I'm sure he hasn't been too clean. Just his name should tell you enough: Sancho. What kind of name is Sancho?

PACHUCO: *¡ORALE!* (*Four women enter stage and stand behind him.*)

PUERTO RICAN GIRL: *Oye, coño*, where have you been, huh? You told me you had to go to a funeral and you've been gone for two weeks now. *Ni una llamada desgraciado.* Oh no. *A mi no me haces estas cosas, chico.* (*Exits.*)

SANCHO: I don't know who she is.

BLONDE GIRL: Oh my god, Sancho. Like you were like the first Mexican I loved. How could you, like, lie to me? Oh my god, gag me with a *churro.* (*Exits.*)

CHOLA: (*She's pregnant.*) This is your baby, Sancho. (*Exits.*)

SANCHO: What?

ADELITA: *¡Que viva Zapata! Y tu mentiroso*, you're lucky I'm fighting a revolution. (*Exits.*)

SANCHO: This can't be true. It's a nightmare. It's a setup.

PACHUCO: Yes, so was the O.J. Simpson trial, something for us to file. *¿Que pasa, vato?* It looks like you're a mess of distress. Aren't you, Sancho? *Ponte trucha. El condón* also protects you from getting your *ruca* pregnant. Are you ready to be a father, Sancho? Are you ready to be a mother, Hildrina? (*A baby falls on their lap and you hear a baby crying in the background.*)

HILDRINA: I don't even know how to change a diaper.

SANCHO: Oh no, man. Baby throw up makes me sick. This can't happen to me. Please, I'm not ready.

PACHUCO: Well, are you ready to meet my friends? *Orale.* (*All the diseases come out. Each disease goes to center stage.*) HERPES, SYPHILLIS, GENITAL WARTS, GONORRHEA, CHLAMYDIA, HIV/AIDS. (*Each disease can create their lines. When they're all done,* Pachuco *snaps his fingers.*) *Orale.* (*They all disappear and take the baby with them.*) *Orale.* Sometimes we don't think of the consequences until we run into fences. If you're not ready to be a father then don't be with another. Let's all work together to stop unwanted pregnancy and also from spreading sexually transmitted diseases. *Orale.* Use your *mente* before you create more g*ente. Y trucha con la carucha. Nos vemos al ratón, jamón. Orale.*

(*End of* acto.)

In 1999, after a show at the Centro Cultural de la Raza we were approached by a woman who worked for the City of Chula Vista. She was interested in hiring us to promote the 2000 Census. We were then hired to create sketches and perform them throughout Chula Vista to promote the Census in the Latino community. They focused on the importance of being counted as a community in order to have certain resources allocated to Latinos. Our sketches included "Super Census" (the wrestler) written by myself and two enthusiastic cheerleaders based on the two cheerleaders from Saturday Night Live written by Cristina Nuñez. Media coverage on the project included an article in the San Diego Union Tribune and other local Latino newpapers.

San Diego Union Tribune, March 18, 2000.
The caption read: **Trolley talk** - *Census 2000, played by Jessie Payan (center), told Theresa Dahdah (right) and riders on the trolley the importance of filling out census forms.*

Teatro Izcalli

Chula Vista the stage for census performers

The San Diego Union Tribune; San Diego, Calif.;
Mar 18, 2000; Samuel Autman;

CHULA VISTA -- A motley crew of seven people wearing shiny garments bursts onto the San Diego Trolley at the H Street station, interrupting what had been a routine trip for most passengers.

Alicia Chavez-Arteaga, attempting to look older, walks to the center of the wobbling train with Hector Villegas, whose exaggerated moustache swallows his mouth. She leans over to him and whispers in Spanish the story of a Mexican woman whose five children were hauled away in a government car after she filled out a census form.

Suddenly "Super Census 2000," a man in a sparkling silver cape, interrupts them and debunks the fictitious tale. He says census information cannot be used for deportation or to hurt families. It is intended to help, he says.

"We aren't the cops, the FBI, the INS or Army guys," exclaim two cheerleaders. "We don't want money. Only your time. It's just a form, for you to sign!"

These people are actors with the Census 2000 Street Theater. Hired by the city of Chula Vista, they have been roaming and performing poignant and humorous skits in English and Spanish in area schools and community centers, on street corners and any place they can get an audience. They can be seen at 1 p.m. today at the Otay Recreational Center at 3554 Main St. during a Census 2000 awareness campaign.

By April 9, the troupe will have done more than 100 performances, all intended to demystify the Census Bureau and persuade citizens and noncitizens to turn in their census forms and be counted.

Earlier this week, the bureau mailed short or long census forms to every address in the nation. It is asking that everyone complete and return them immediately so the government can conduct its decennial count of all the people, as mandated in the U.S. Constitution. Census data are used in distributing some federal funds and to reconfigure water, school and legislative districts.

In the 1990 census, minority populations were disproportionately undercounted for numerous reasons. Some members of minorities did not trust the government, and others did not see a need to return the forms. Whatever the reason, the result was an estimated undercount of minority populations that ranged from 2 percent to nearly 5 percent.

One of the biggest problems for Latinos in San Diego County is the fear that the very personal data on the long form will be used to deport illegal immigrants. But neither the Congress, Immigration Naturalization Service, Internal Revenue Service or any other agency can access the 2000 Census data until the year 2072, according to federal law.

commissioned works

Macedonio Arteaga Jr., 32, head of the troupe, understands why people would be fearful of being shipped back to Mexico and of the breakup of

139

families. He was born in Michoacan, Mexico, and his family lived in San Diego County illegally for years.

Arteaga, a health educator, runs a program called the Circle of Men at the Logan Heights Family Health Center.

"You might come home from school and your parents aren't there," he said of his childhood memories. "I was not allowed to play soccer or any sport until I was bigger. My mom was afraid they (INS) would come and get me." Arteaga, who said his family is now legal and his application for citizenship is pending, approaches these census skits with a missionary zeal.

Before each performance, he appears sporting a blue mask, much like the one worn by a legendary Mexican wrestler, the Blue Demon. He said the blue mask is an attention grabber and a friendly face to most Mexicans.
"It was very cool," said Cindy Sepulveda, 14, a trolley passenger.
Added Joyce Hudgens, a tourist from West Virginia, "It was good. It really got people's attention."

Jeri Gulbransen, a spokeswoman for the city of Chula Vista, said the $25,000 that pays for the troupe's performances comes from the San Diego Association of Governments. Cities throughout the region have used SANDAG money to promote the census because the higher their population the bigger the slice of federal money that will come into their communities.
"I love this idea," Gulbransen said. "It reaches out to people. It goes where they are, to people's neighborhoods, in restaurants while they are eating and on the trolley while they are going to work.

"It really is touching the people who may have fears about being counted or just might not think about it. People are now asking them for census forms."

Teatro Izcalli

140

SUPER CENSUS
By Macedonio Arteaga Jr.

CHARACTERS:

SUPER CENSUS - A Mexican wrestler wearing a mask, cape, pants, and a shirt that says Super Census.
COMADRE - Woman in her fifties with long braids.
COMPADRE - Mexican cowboy with a giant mustache, gold chains, boots, and a hat.

(Comadre is *at a laundry mat washing clothes.*)
COMADRE: I can't believe how dirty these kids are. And that husband of mine. Just look at this. (*She pulls out some dirty boxers.*)
      Boy I wish somebody showed him what being clean is.
COMPADRE: (*Enters riding a broom-horse.* Quebradita *music plays in the background.*) Hi *comadre*, how are you? (*He gets off his horse.*)
COMADRE: Very good, *compadre*, just washing your *compadre's* dirty underwear.
COMPADRE: Ay, *comadre*. That's TMI.

COMADRE: TMI?

COMPADRE: Too much information, *comadre. Demasiada información.* But *comadre*, I have to tell you something.

COMADRE: Oh no! But *compadre*, if it's gossip, I'd rather not hear it. Remember we're not going to gossip anymore.

COMPADRE: No *comadre*. This isn't gossip. It's vital information. You know, like the internet.

COMADRE: Well, if it's vital information, you can tell me. But no gossip. I'm going to the CRC, you know, the *Chisme* Rehab Center.

COMPADRE: I already went through that program, *comadre.* That's why I only give out important information, not gossip. Look *comadre*, let me tell you. Listen to what happened. Last night, the census people came over. You know what the census is, right?

COMADRE: Yes. The census is like the INS, right?

COMPADRE: Yes, yes *comadre*. Look. They came to Doña Choncha's house and they counted all of her kids, you know, Chuche, Rafa, el Pulga, her daughter Chona, Zopo and Aranita. Right after they counted them, they rounded them all up and took them in a big car. They still haven't returned, no one knows what happened to them.

COMADRE: *Ay Virgen de Guadalupe* and all of the saints from my *pueblo!* Look *compadre*, I also heard that the census people came over to Don Chito's house and when they counted everyone, they took away their medical benefits and they threw Don Chito in jail because he ran over Don Juan's dog five years ago.

COMPADRE: Yes, yes I heard that too. It's true. I already told my kids that if the census people come, not to open the door and to run and hide underneath the beds.

SUPER CENSUS: (Super Censo *jumps out in front of them.*) Hey gossipers, stop!

COMADRE AND COMPADRE: It's Super Census!

COMADRE: (*The* Compadre *hides behind* his Comadre.) Don't get any closer, Super Census. I'm trained to defend myself from evil people like you.

COMPADRE: (*While hiding behind the* Comadre.) It wasn't me! It was the gossipy *comadre*. I don't gossip anymore, I only pass on vital information.

SUPER CENSUS: Listen, bunch of gossipers. I come to tell you the truth. The census is here to help you. The *migra* won't come to get you and you won't be reported to the police.

Teatro Izcalli COMPADRE: (*He stands up.*) Well, then, it's a good thing you came, Super Census. I was just telling the *comadre* about all of the gossip that the people have been saying about the census. All lies, I tell you! Lies!

142

You know how people can talk.

COMADRE: (*She turns towards her* Compadre *and hits him with a sock.*) You're just like your *compadre*. Well, Super Census. Now that you're here, dressed in tights and all, tell me. Why is the census so important?

SUPER CENSUS: (Super Census *does a cartwheel.*) Well, Mrs. Gossip...

COMADRE: (*She throws a sock at him and he kicks it in the air.*) I don't gossip, Super Census. I only pass on vital information. (*She looks at the audience.*)

SUPER CENSUS: Yeah, sure. Let me explain. It's very important that you get counted and that you cooperate because the information that you give will be used to determine which communities need new schools, services for the elderly, and other essential things.

COMPADRE: And how do they count us? Like this: one, two, three? (*He's showing the wrong number of fingers.*)

COMADRE: (*Hits* Compadre *with a sock again then turns to* Super Census.) Tell us, Super Census. How do they count us?

SUPER CENSUS: You'll be given a questionnaire that will only take about ten minutes to fill out. All the information that you will give will be completely confidential.

COMADRE: Well, I'm glad you told us. Now we won't be scared of the census people when they come knocking on our door.

SUPER CENSUS: I'm glad this is all cleared up. Now you can relay this "vital information" to all of your friends. But I'd like to ask you a question.

COMPADRE AND COMADRE: (*Both.*) What is it?

SUPER CENSUS: Is it true that Susana, from apartment ten, left her husband with their ten children?

COMPADRE AND COMADRE: (*Both gasp dramatically.*) Super Censo, we don't gossip.

SUPER CENSUS: No, it's not gossip. It's vital information.

COMADRE: Well, in that case, let me tell you. Not only did she leave him, but she stole his car and she ran off with the mailman. (*Exit stage gossiping.*)

(*End of* acto.)

Census 2000. Back left: Macedonio Arteaga Jr., Ricky Medina, Alicia Chavez, Hector Villegas. Front left: Cristina Nuñez, Jesse Payan, and Iyari Arteaga. Photo by Laura Embry.

Census 2000. Iyari Arteaga and Victor Chavez Jr. Photo by Jaime Diego Chavez.

Teatro Izcalli

SUPER CENSO
Por Macedonio Arteaga Jr.

PERSONAJES:

COMADRE - Una mujer de unos cincuenta años. Trae ropa para lavar.

COMPADRE - Un hombre de unos cincuenta años también. Está vestido de vaquero tiene un bigote muy grande.

(*La* Comadre *esta lavando ropa en una lavandería.*)

COMADRE: No puedo creer que cochinos son estos niños. ¡Hay Dios mío! ¿Y ese esposo? Mire nomás. que cochino! (*Saca unos calzoncillos muy sucios.*)

COMPADRE: (*El* Compadre *entra en un caballito de madera. Se escucha música de quebradita al fondo.*) Hola comadre. ¿Cómo esta? (*Se baja del caballito.*)

COMADRE: Muy bien compadre, pues aquí nomás lavando los calzones de su compadre cochino.

COMPADRE: Ay que comadre. Eso es DI.

COMADRE: ¿Que es eso?

COMPADRE: Pues demasiada información comadre. *Too much*

information, pero comadre, le tengo que decir unas cosas.

COMADRE: ¡Hay no! Pero compadre, si es chisme no quiero saber. Acuérdese que ya no somos chismosos.

COMPADRE: No, comadre pero este no es chisme, es información vital. Ya sabe, como el internet.

COMADRE: Bueno, si es información, sí me puede decir. Pero nada de chisme. Estoy en el CRC, o sea el centro de rehabilitación de los chismosos.

COMPADRE: Pues yo ya pasé por ese curso comadre, por eso nomás doy información importante, no es chisme. Mire comadre, deje decirle. Mire lo que pasó. Anoche vino la gente del censo. ¿Sabe que es el censo, verdad?

COMADRE: Sí. El censo es como la migra, ¿verdad?

COMPADRE: Sí, sí comadre, mire. Vinieron a la casa de Doña Choncha y contaron a todos sus hijos, a Chuche, Rafa, El Pulga, su hija la Chona, al Zopo y la Arañita. Y despues de que los contaron se los llevaron a todos en un carro grande. Y no han regresado. Nadie sabe donde estan.

COMADRE: Válgame Dios, la Virgen de Guadalupe y todos los santos de mi pueblo. Mire compadre yo también oí que a la casa de Don Chito, vinieron los del censo y cuando contaron a toda la gente les quitaron su Medical y metieron a Don Chito a la cárcel porque hace cinco años atropelló al perrito de Don Juan, el paletero.

COMPADRE: Ay Dios mío. Sí, sí oí eso. Es verdad. Ya sé, si vienen los del censo a mi casa, mis hijos saben que no deben de abrir la puerta y correrán a esconderse debajo de la cama.

SUPER CENSO: (*Súper Censo brinca enfrente de ellos.*) Raza chismosa, ¡Deténganse!

COMPADRE Y COMADRE: ¡El Súper Censo!

COMADRE: (*El Compadre se esconde detrás de la Comadre.*) No se acerque más. Yo estoy entrenada para defenderme de los malos como usted.

COMPADRE: (*Al esconderse detrás de la Comadre.*) Amá, Amá. Yo no fui, fue la comadre chismosa. Yo ya no digo chismes, nomás información vital.

SUPER CENSO: ¡Atención bola de chismosos! ¡Vengo a decirles la verdad! El Censo está para ayudarles. (*Saca los letreros.*) No se los va llevar la migra. No serán reportados a la policía. (*Súper Censo rompe los letreros.*)

COMPADRE: (*El Compadre se para.*) Pues que bueno

que vino, Súper Censo. Le estaba diciendo a la comadre todo el chisme que la gente está diciendo del censo. Puras mentiras, Súper Censo. ¡Puras mentiras! Ya sabe como es la gente.

COMADRE: (*Ella se voltea y le da un calcetinazo.*) Es usted igual que su compadre. Bueno, Súper Censo, ya que esta aquí vestido muy de medias y con todo ese relajo que trae puesto. ¿Y porque es tan importante todo esto lo del censo?

SUPER CENSO: (Súper Censo *se da una maroma.*) Bueno señora chismosa…

COMADRE: (*Le tira un calcetín.*) Yo no soy chismosa, Súper Censo. Solo pasó información vital. (*Mira al público.*)

SUPER CENSO: Sí, chuy. Miren. Dejen, les explico. Es muy importante que los cuenten porque la información se usa para determinar cuales comunidades necesitan nuevas escuelas, servicios para los ancianos y mucho más.

COMPADRE: ¿Y como nos cuentan? ¿Así uno, dos, tres, cuatro? (*Cuenta mal con los dedos.*)

COMADRE: (*Le da otro calcetinazo al* Compadre.) Si será. No le doy otro calcetinazo porque prefiero evitar la fatiga. A ver Súper Choni, digo, Súper Censo. Díganos, ¿como nos cuentan?

SUPER CENSO: Se les dará un cuestionario que solo tomará de diez a quince minutos. Toda la información que se dé es confidencial.

COMADRE: Pues que bueno que nos dijo. Ahora no le tendremos miedo a la gente del censo cuando nos toquen la puerta.

SUPER CENSO: Que bueno que se aclaro todo esto. Ahora ya pueden pasar la "información vital" a todos sus amigos. Pero quiero hacerles una pregunta.

COMPADRE Y COMADRE: ¿Cuál es?

SUPER CENSO: ¿Es verdad que Susana, la del apartamento diez abandonó a su marido con todos los hijos?

COMPADRE Y COMADRE: (*Los dos se muestran sorprendidos y se tapan la boca.*) Súper Censo, nosotros no somos chismosos.

SUPER CENSO: No, eso no es chisme. Es información vital.

COMADRE: Ah bueno, en ese caso. Fíjese que no solo lo dejó, pero le robó el carro y se fue con el cartero. (*Se van chismeando del escenario.*)

(*Fin.*)

In 2003 we were hired by the Chicano Federation with funds from the 0-5 Commission to perform sketches around San Diego to educate parents on raising children in the critical ages of 0-5 years old. I was given some videos and books and then asked to write a script that would be appealing to the Mexican-American community. All of the *actos* were written in Spanish with the help of Marta Flores who was patient enough to help us with the proper translation. Despite the comedy, the audiences were able to receive the important parenting messages we needed to convey. One of the highlights of this project was that we had the opportunity to hire a Chicano legend, Ramon "Chunky" Sanchez to work with us.

ÉL BEBÉ 0 a 5
Por Macedonio Arteaga Jr. *

PERSONAJES:

DOCTORA - Saco blanco, estetoscopio, cuaderno con papeles.
MAMÁ - Tiene un juguete del Santo Enmascarado de Plata en su bolsa.
PAPÁ- En sus cuarentas.

(*La* Mamá *y el* Papá *estan en la oficina de la* Doctora.)
DOCTORA: Familia Rota se puede sentar por favor. Parece señora que usted tiene algo que llamamos escandolitis.
MAMÁ: Ave María Purísima sin pecado concebido, Jesús de Veracruz, ruega por nosotros El Santo Enmascarado de Plata. ¿Ay doctora pero que enfermedad es esa?
PAPÁ: Te dije vieja que eres muy escandalosa.

DOCTORA: Bueno señora esta enfermedad es muy peligrosa y se puede transmitir nomás con ver a otra persona.
MAMÁ: Pero doctora, vengo a un chequeo a ver si estoy embarazada.
DOCTORA: (*Esta viendo sus papeles.*) O disculpe señora, estos no son sus

resultados son de otra paciente.

MAMÁ: Oh gracias Santo Enmascarado de Plata. (*Saca un muñeco del santo de su bolsa y le da un beso. Se lo enseña al* Papá.) Dile gracias al Santo. Dale un beso al Santo, viejo.

PAPÁ: ¿Un beso? Como le voy a dar un beso, vieja. Si ni a tí te doy besos. Como le voy a dar un beso al Santo. ¿Que no entiendes que el Santo fue luchador?

MAMÁ: ¡Que le des un beso, te dije!

PAPÁ: (*Viendo a la doctora y luego con vergüenza le da un beso al Santo.*)

MAMÁ: Gracias, viejo. Por eso te quiero tanto, mi chocolate panzón.

DOCTORA: Ahem, ahem.

MAMÁ: Oh sí, doctora.

DOCTORA: Mire sus resultados de su prueba de embarazo son positivos.

MAMÁ Y PAPÁ: Estamos embarazados, estamos embarazados.

(Papá *se desmaya y la* Mamá *le sopla aire con su bolsa.*)

DOCTORA: (Doctora *camina al frente del escenario.*) Hola yo soy la Doctora Saca Bebé. Les voy hablar de algo muy importante. Ya que la Familia Rota va a tener su primer hijo es importante que entiendan algunas cosas. Es muy importante que una mamá se cuide y empiece con un chequeo y luego continué con todas su citas prenatales. Recuerde que tiene que evitar los cigarros, las drogas y el alcohol pare tener un bebé saludable. También tome todas las vitaminas prenatales que le dé la doctora. Trate de comer lo más saludable posible. No se espante cuando suba más de peso. Es normal que la mujer suba de 25 a 30 libras durante su embarazo. Gracias y los veo en su próxima cita.

(*Fin.*)

149

ÉL BEBÉ NACE

Por Macedonio Arteaga Jr.

PERSONAJES:

MAMÁ - Embarazada.
PAPÁ - Tiene guante de béisbol.
HADA MADRINA - Vestida de hada madrina.

(*Acto comienza cuando entra la* Mamá *gritando.*)
MAMÁ: ¡Ya se me rompió el agua!! ¡Viejo! ¡Viejo! ¡Ya!!
PAPÁ: (*Entra al escenario con pánico.*) ¡Aaahhh! ¡Agua!! ¡Me ahogo, vieja!!
MAMÁ: Cálmese viejo escandaloso. Ya ve y trae las cosas necesarias para el hospital.
PAPÁ: Ropa de cambio, pañales, toallas. Tengo todo. (*Se sale.*)
MAMÁ: (*Regresa el* Papá.) ¿Se te olvidó algo?
PAPÁ: ¡Sí, sí! ¿Pero no sé que se me olvida?
MAMÁ: ¿¡Y yo que menso?!

Teatro Izcalli   PAPÁ: ¡Ah sí! ¿Y él bebé? ¿Dónde esta él bebé?
MAMÁ: ¡Julio, él bebé todavía no nace! (*Empieza a gritar.*) Agh, ya. ¡Ya! Ya no puedo. ¡Ay dios mío! ¡Ya sáquenme a este niño. Ya va salir este muchacho! Ya no vamos a llegar al hospital.

150

¡Apúrate! Unas toallas y agua caliente. ¡Julio tú me hiciste esto! Nunca, nunca me vuelvas a tocar. Nunca Julio. Agh! ¿Por qué nosotras? ¿Por qué la mujer? ¿Por qué no a estos hombres miserables que no sufren nunca? ¡Lo más que sufren es cuando su malvado equipo de fútbol pierde! ¿Por qué dios, por qué? ¡Ahgggg!! ¡Julio!

PAPÁ: Espérate, espérate un momento mi amor.

VOZ: (*Se oye un juego de béisbol.*) ¡Un gran batazo al jardín izquierdo corriendo hasta la barda y qué gran atrapada por Sosa! (*En ese momento el Papá corre con un guante en su mano.*) ¡Qué gran atrapada! (*El Papá atrapa al bebé.*)

MAMÁ: Mira, ¡es igualito a tí!

PAPÁ: Sí, ¿verdad? Y también nació con pañal, ¡que suave! Pero mujer, ¿ahora que hacemos? Es nuestro primer hijo.

MAMÁ: Bueno viejo, tenemos dos opciones. Podemos asistir a clases para ser buenos padres o puedes traer a mi mamá para que se quede aquí unos años para que nos ayude.

PAPÁ: Deja pensarlo. ¿La suegra aquí? ¿O las clases? ¿La suegra o las clases? Me la pones muy difícil pero por lo pronto hay que tomar unas clases, ¿que no? Ahorita mismo voy a escribirnos. Antes de que llegue la suegra. (*Sale corriendo el Papá.*)

HADA MADRINA: (*Entra al escenario.*) Hola, yo soy la hada madrina de la Familia Rota. Y estoy aquí para informarles sobre algunas cosas muy importantes acerca del cuidado de su bebé. (Mamá *está actuando las recomendaciones.*) Como por ejemplo, durante los primeros meses algunos bebés se han muerto de algo llamado *SIDS* en español es el Síndrome de Muerte Infantil Súbita. Lo poco que sabemos para tratar de evitar la muerte de *SIDS* es dormir a su bebé de espalda. Los bebés no se van a ahogar si están de espalda. Tampoco use cobijas o cobertores con pelusa para cubrir a su bebé. No ponga cosas como juguetes de peluche almohadas o almohadillas en la cuna. (Mamá *tira unos monos de peluche fuera de la cuna.*) También sabemos que SIDS ocurre más cuando en casa hay gente que fuma. El humo del cigarro es muy peligroso y con el tiempo también puede hacer al bebé más susceptible a infecciones, gripas, alergias y hasta puede desarrollar el Asma. Ahora, cuando le esté cambiando el pañal a su bebé asegúrese que siempre lo esté viendo, el bebé se puede voltear de la cama muy rápido y caerse. Fíjese que el niño no pueda agarrar el talco. Algunos bebés se han muerto simplemente por oler o tragar el talco. Y por último, recuerden que el cuello del bebé es muy delicado y en los primeros meses uno siempre tiene que sostenerles el cuello. Ay me están hablando al beeper, ya nació otro bebé. Adiós.

(*Fin.*)

Él Bebé Nace. Claudia Cuevas and Ramon "Chunky" Sanchez.
Photo by Alicia Chavez

Teatro Izcalli

SALUD DE LOS NIÑOS
Por Macedonio Arteaga Jr.

PERSONAJES:

HADA MADRINA
MAMÁ
PAPÁ
HIJO
DOCTORA

(*Acto comienza con la* Hada Madrina *hablando.*)

HADA: Quiero que todos tomen un momento para acordarse que lindo y no
tan doloroso fue el nacimiento de su bebé. Es la experiencia que
se le puede olvidar a una familia. Bueno, ahora es muy importante
empezar a hablar como criar a un niño saludable.
Los estudios nos enseñan que los primeros cinco
años del bebé son los más importantes de su vida.
Son muy importantes porque es cuando el cerebro se desarrolla más
rápido.

MAMÁ: (*Está viendo que el* Papá *juega con el* Hijo *haciéndole unas caras muy mensas.*) ¿Y si el cerebro nunca se desarrolla pasando los cinco anos? (*Apunta al* Papá.)

HADA: Bueno, eso es otro tema. Ay que ver lo importante en esta parte de la vida del niño. Nunca es muy temprano para empezar a leerle a su niño. Les aconsejamos que les lean a los niños desde cuando estén en la matriz.

MAMÁ: (*Empieza a leerle una revista al* Hijo). Mira mijo, María Ester se fue con Diego y se iba a casar con Claudio. Válgame dios.

HADA: También uno puede cantarle canciones a su niño. (*El* Papá *canta una canción de Vicente Fernández. La* Mamá *lo empuja y empieza a cantar también. Los dos empiezan a cantar más alto tratando de obtener la atención del* Hijo. *La* Hada Madrina *mueve su "barra mágica" para que paren de cantar y los dos no paran.*) Por favor. Ya paren de cantar. ¡Ya! (*No paran.*) ¡Por favor, ya basta!

MAMÁ: Pero señora, tenga más paciencia.

HADA: Ahem, ahem, disculpen. Que voz tan linda tienen los dos. Bueno, continuamos. También recuerden que es importante jugar con su niño.

PAPÁ: Oh sí maestra, yo sé eso. (*Corre y agarra una pelota de fútbol. El* Hijo *se para a jugar.*) Agarra la pelota. Tú eres el portero. Para la pelota así. Saca las manos bien, bien. (*El* Papá *patea la pelota y le pega al* Hijo *y lo tumba.*) ¡¡Gol! ¡Gol! Es gol. No llores, los hombres no lloran. (*Los personajes pausan.*)

HADA: Es importante jugar juegos que no lo vayan a lastimar. Y por favor, hay que enseñarles a los niños que desde chicos los hombres pueden lloran y expresar sus sentimientos.

PAPÁ: A ver mijo, ¿por qué lloras?

HIJO: Por que tu patear pelota y duele aquí.

PAPÁ: Lo siento mijo. Fue un accidente. Ya no vuelvo a patear la pelota así.

MAMA: A ver mijo, ven y siéntate conmigo.

HADA: También puede darle pinturas y crayones a su niño para que empiece a pintar, colorear y dibujar. Pero claro, ya que estén más grandecitos.

PAPÁ: Mira mijo, puedes dibujar una persona así.

HIJO: ¿Así papí?

PAPÁ: Sí, está muy bien mijo. Muy bonito.

HADA: El cuidado de los dientes de su hijo es muy importante. Por ejemplo, no duerma a su bebé con una botella. Sus dientes tienen que ser lavados desde los seis meses y así puede ayudar a su bebé tener dientes saludables. Y también no deje que su niño tome de la botella después de los doce meses. Pregúntenle al doctor sobre el florido para proteger los dientes de su niño.

Teatro Izcalli

Lleven a su niño al dentista en el primer año, o si notan algunas manchas. A los dos años empiece a enseñarle a su niño como lavarse los dientes.

MAMÁ: ¿Te acuerdas como te enseñe a lavarte los dientes?

HIJO: Sí. (*El* Hijo *sale del escenario.*)

MAMÁ: (*Marca el teléfono.*) Bueno. Hola comadre. Sí, ya lo ví. No me diga. A ver, permíteme. Mijo. (*Llamándole al* Hijo.) ¿Te pusiste pasta en los dientes?

HIJO: Sí. (*Sale al escenario con pasta de dientes por toda la cara.*)

MAMÁ: ¡Ay dios mío! ¡Muchacho! Comadre luego le hablo (*El* Hijo *empieza a llorar y se va corriendo.*)

HADA: Sin gritarle al niño. Acuérdese que está aprendiendo y además no hizo nada malo. No es necesario gritarles a los niños por cosas tan sencillas. Por ejemplo, si tiran un vaso de leche por accidente el niño no debe de tener miedo por algo tan sencillo. Y también permita que su hijo empiece a comer solo antes de que cumpla su primer año. Seguramente hará un cochinero, pero está bien. Déjelo que coma solo. Claro con supervision. Así aprenden los niños.
(*Entra el* Hijo *rascándose la cabeza.*)

MAMÁ: No me digas que tienes piojos. Ahorita mismo te voy a rasurar la cabeza.

HADA: Señora, no hay que ser tan drástica. Hay champús para eso. Consulte con su doctor sobre otras alternativas. Y recuerda no mande a su niño a la escuela. Los piojos se transmiten fácilmente cuando se comparten los peines, las cachuchas, o las chamarras.

MAMÁ: Haber déjame revisarte bien. No tienes nada.

HADA: Durante los primeros cinco años su hijo tiene que recibir las vacunas requeridas por el estado de California. De nuevo vamos con la Familia Rota a su visita al doctor. Recuerden que es necesario explicarle al niño lo que va pasar en su chequeo físico. Por ejemplo, puede explicarle que las vacunas son importantes pare que no se enferme gravemente.

MAMÁ: Mijo, no te va a doler la vacuna. Estas vacunas son muy importantes porque si no te las dan, te puedes enfermar mucho.

HIJO: ¿Enfermar mucho?

MAMÁ: Sí mijo. ¿Te acuerdas como se enfermó tu perico, Chocho? ¿Te acuerdas que se puso tieso y empezó a temblar y luego le salió algo muy feo de la boca? ¿Te acuerdas mijo?

HIJO: Sí.

MAMÁ: Bueno, si no te damos tus vacunas te puede pasar lo mismo.

DOCTORA: (*Entra.*) Hola Señora Rota. ¿Cómo está?

MAMÁ: Bien, bien. Mi hijo, Rotito.

DOCTORA: Hola, Rotito. ¿Te explicaron un poco tus padres lo que te vamos a hacer hoy?

HIJO: Sí, dijo mi mamá que me voy a poner tieso como mi perico.

DOCTORA: ¡¿Cómo?! ¿De qué estás hablando niño?

MAMÁ: No, doctora. Yo le dije que le tenemos que dar estas vacunas para que no se enferme como su perico, Chocho. Se nos murió hace poco.

DOCTORA: Muy bien, ya entiendo. ¿Estás listo? (La Doctora *saca una jeringa grande.*) No te va a doler. No tengas miedo. Una para la Hepatitis y otra para el Polio.

MAMÁ: Si quieres llorar está bien mijo.

HIJO: No, estoy bien. Sí me dolió, pero poquito.

DOCTORA: Okay, Rotito es todo por hoy. Al rato tienes que regresar para el DTP Meningitis, Varicela, Sarampión y Viruela. No puedes ir a la escuela hasta que te demos todas estas vacunas.

HIJO: Para que no me ponga tieso como mi perico, Chocho.

DOCTORA: Sí, para que no te pongas tieso como tu perico, Chocho.

(*Fin.*)

WALTERMALCRIADO: LA DISCIPLINA
Por Macedonio Arteaga Jr.

PERSONAJES:

MAMÁ
PAPÁ
NIÑA
NIÑO
WALTER
HADA MADRINA
DIABLO
POLICIA

(*Acto comienza con la voz de la* Hada Madrina.)

HADA: Miren que bien se portó Rotito con el doctor. Pero como nosotros sabemos eso no siempre es el caso. ¿Verdad? ¿Qué es la disciplina? ¿Cuándo uno piensa en la disciplina, ¿qué es lo que uno piensa? ¿Si se acuerdan como los disciplinaron sus padres? (*Saca un cinto o una vara de árbol.*) Vamos en vivo con el hijo de la Familia Rota

157

para hacerle una entrevista sobre el tema de la disciplina.

NIÑO: Mi mamá cuando se enoja me hace así. Una vez me jaló la oreja y se me cayó la oreja y mi tío que trabaja de jardinero me la tuvo que pegar otra vez. Es verdad.

HADA: ¿Y cómo te sientes cuando tu mamá te hace eso?

NIÑO: No me gusta, yo digo ¡*ouch*! Y lloro mucho.

HADA: Lo escucharon en vivo desde la casa de la Familia Rota. El niño Juan Rota nos dice que cuando le jalan la oreja, él dice *ouch*.

NIÑA: También me pega con un cinto o me grita bien feo y yo le tengo miedo por que pienso que me va pegar más duro.

HADA: Escuchen la voz de Juanito Roto, un niño que sufre el dolor de la disciplina que está causando más daño que bien. Hay alternativas. Hay otras maneras de disciplinar a su hijo o hija. Estudios indican que los niños que son disciplinados físicamente la mayoría de los casos toman su agresión en contra de otros niños y también en contra de los adultos. A la vez, este tipo de disciplina puede afectar a los niños en la escuela y en su desarrollo social. Para aprender más sobre el tema de la disciplina vamos en vivo con el que si sabe más de la disciplina. ¡Walter Malcriado!

WALTER: Hola. Hola. Walter Malcriado aquí con ustedes. Sagitario este es tu mes. Vas a ver tus chones favoritos, los que perdiste la última vez que anduviste en las montañas, explorando el mundo. Leo, Leo pero que feo. No te preocupes, las cosas van a mejorar para ti. Aunque te vas a quebrar tu dedo chico en un accidente de golf. Bueno hoy estamos aquí para hablar de la disciplina. Ay sí, creciendo mi mamá siempre me decía malcriado para acá, mis maestras, la comunidad, todos me dicen malcriado, malcriado, malcriado. Hasta que un día le pregunté a mi mamá. ¿Por qué todos me dicen malcriado? Y ella me dijo. ¿Cómo que porque te dicen malcriado? Menso. ¡Si ese es tu apellido! Desde ese tiempo, decidí hacer algo para todos los niños malcriados del mundo. Es cuando creí mi propio video. Se llama, "Como Disciplinar al Niño Malcriado Sin Darle Cintarazos, Jalarle el Pelo, Pellizcarlo, o Gritarles en Público. Y ahora vamos a ver un poco de este video. ¿Qué es lo que debemos de hacer cuando un niño se tira y hace un berrinche en la tienda? Vamos a ver con nuestra familia.

NIÑA: (*Entra al escenario con su* Papá.) Yo quiero ese juguete. Yo quiero eso. Papí, papí cómprame eso. Sí papí. Sí, sí, papí, sí.

PAPÁ: No. Te digo que no tengo dinero. ¡No!

NIÑA: Tú eres feo. ¡Agggghhh! (*Se tira al piso.*)

PAPÁ: (*Papá hace lo mismo tirándose al piso.*) ¡Agggghhh! (*Se levante del piso.*) Niña mala. Niña mala. Eres una niña muy mala.

WALTER: En esta situación ¿Cuál es la respuesta correcta?

158

a). Actuar igual que su hija.

b). Decirle que el Diablo se la va llevar.

c). La Policía se la va llevar.

d). Ninguna de las respuestas.

PAPÁ: Te va llevar el Diablo. (*Se aparece el* Diablo.)

DIABLO: No sé donde está mi mamá. (*Se desaparece.*)

PAPÁ: Te va llevar la Policía. (*Se aparece un* Policía *comiendo una dona.*)

POLICIA: No puede ser, es mi última dona. (*Se desaparece.*)

WALTER: Asustar a su hija no es una manera de disciplinarla. El temor a los padres o de que se la va llevar el diablo, puede causar mas daño de lo que uno piensa. Algunas otras estrategias incluyen, preguntarle a la niña, por qué está llorando.

PAPÁ: Mija, ¿por qué estás llorando?

NIÑA: (*Llorando.*) Porque tú no me compras lo que quiero.

PAPÁ: ¿Por eso lloras? Bueno pues, sigue llorando. Yo aquí me espero hasta que termines de llorar. (*Los dos salen del escenario.*)

WALTER: Otra cosa que uno puede hacer, es llevarse la niña al carro y quedarse con ella hasta que deje de llorar. Cuando los niños hacen algo que no es correcto en la casa uno les puede dar un "Time Out" o descanso temporal. Se hace lo siguiente, tomen al niño y póngalo en una área designada "descanso temporal" para que tengan tiempo de pensar en lo que hizo. Si llora, espere a que termine de llorar. Cuando termine de llorar pregúntele si sabe porque lo puso en "Time Out". Es muy difícil enseñarle al niño que no pegue cuando se enoja. Si cuando usted se enoja con el, usted le pega. Los siguientes puntos son muy importantes cuando usted disciplina a su hijo. Asegúrese que su hijo entienda bien, que él no es un niño malo, sino lo que está haciendo no es bueno. Por ejemplo.

MAMÁ: (*Entra al escenario con el* Niño.) Mijo te quiero mucho no eres un niño malo pero tus acciones no son buenas y pueden afectar a otros y a ti mismo. Te voy a dar un descanso por que le tiraste piedras a Rafita y le pegaste en la cabeza. Me entiendes porque te estoy dando tiempo afuera.

NIÑO: Sí, porque yo le tiré piedras a Rafita y eso no es bueno. Lo puede lastimar muy feo.

MAMÁ: Sí, mijo.

WALTER: Muy bien. Hay que hacer la disciplina con amor. Gritando y perdiendo el control no cambia el comportamiento del niño. Lo que va a pasar es que el niño siga gritando y maltratando a otros. Un padre que está tratando de enseñar disciplina no lo está haciendo cuando ella o él mismo pierde el control enfrente de otros. Vamos a ver un ejemplo de lo que no se debe de hacer. (*Entra la*

commissioned works

159

Niña *al escenario.*)

NIÑO: ¡Tú estás fea! (*Le tira una muñeca a su hermana.*)

NIÑA: (*Gritando.*) ¡Mamá, me pegó Julio con la muñeca!

MAMÁ: Muchacho, ¿qué estás haciendo? (*Agarra al* Niño *de la oreja y le da un jalón.*) A ver si no te quito esa maña de tirar piedras (*Le da unas nalgadas y el* Niño *se va llorando.*)

WALTER: Recuerde, usted es el adulto. Debe de controlarse y pensar en otras formas de disciplinar a su hijo. ¡Piénselo! Otros consejos que debe de tomar en cuenta son: Si el niño tiene entre 1 y 4 años, no espere que se quede sentado durante toda la cena. No espere que su hijo se termine toda la comida. Ellos saben cuando están llenos. Bueno, soy Walter Malcriado y es todo por hoy.

(*Fin.*)

JUAN ESTASBIEN
Por Macedonio Arteaga Jr.

PERSONAJES:

LOCUTOR
JUAN ESTABIEN
DOÑA ROTA
PAPÁ

(*Se escucha la voz del* Locutor.)

LOCUTOR: Buenas noches y bienvenidos al show de Juan ESTASSSSBIENNN. Y ahora el conductor mas conocido en su casa, un aplauso fuerte para Juan Estasbien.

ESTASBIEN: (*Sale y se cae de frente y luego se levanta.*) Estoy bien, estoy bien. Hola, bienvenidos a otro programa de Juan Estasbien. Ahora tenemos un show muy interesante y lleno de educación para los padres que tienen hijos menores de cinco años de edad.
Pero primero vamos a ver si hay un voluntario que nos ayude con en el escenario. (Doña Rota *levanta la mano.*) Déjenme ver, va a ser

161

difícil escoger a alguien de tanta gente que quiere ser voluntario. Bueno, bueno, usted. (Doña Rota *se apunta a ella misma*.)

DOÑA ROTA: ¿Yo?

ESTASBIEN: Sí, sí, usted.

DOÑA ROTA: Ya sabía que me iba pasar esto. Ayer hablé con Walter Malcriado y me dijo que veía muchas estrellas en mi futuro. Sabía que iba a ser una estrella un día de estos. Lo sabía. ¿Mamá estás viendo? Gracias por tu apoyo.

ESTASBIEN: Bueno, bueno señora vamos a empezar. Aquí están las instrucciónes para usted.

DOÑA ROTA: Gracias señor, gracias.

ESTASBIEN: Miles de niños en los Estadios Unidos se lastiman seriamente o se mueren cada año en este país por cosas que nosotros, como padres, podemos evitar. Ahora vamos a aprender como podemos evitar algunas tragedias y mantener a nuestros hijos seguros desde que nacen. Empecemos con el viaje en el automóvil. Es muy importante que usen un asiento infantil de seguridad para su hijo, cada vez que el niño este dentro de un automóvil. Esta es la ley en California. El bebé debe de estar en el asiento trasero. Revise que la silla esté bien segura cuando siente al bebé. (*Se machuca el dedo en el cinto de seguridad*.) ¡Aaaagggghhhh! ¡Mi dedo! ¡Mi dedo!

DOÑA ROTA: ¿Señor Estasbien?

ESTASBIEN: (*En agonía*.) Sí, sí estoy bien. Estoy bien. Bueno, su bebé debe de usar un asiento infantil de seguridad hasta que su hijo tenga seis años de edad o pese más de 60 libras. (*Doña Rota tiene al bebé en sus brazos*.) Por favor, no cargue a su bebé en sus brazos dentro de un carro. Como su hijo estará en la casa la mayoría del tiempo debe asegurarse que todo esté bien en la casa para evitar accidentes graves. Cuando el bebé ya empiece a gatear hay que ponernos de rodillas para ver lo que ve el bebé. Cuando vea alambres de electricidad sueltos, es buena idea ponerles cinta de aislar y pegarlos junto a la pared, así el bebé no podrá agárralos o jalar lámparas que pueden caer y lastimarlo. También, es muy importante comprar cobertores para cubrir los enchufes. Esto evita el riesgo que un bebé pueda meter su dedo y electrocutarse. (*Mete su dedo por accidente adentro del enchufe y es electrocutado*.)

DOÑA ROTA: Señor Estasbien, ¿está bien?

ESTASBIEN: (*Temblando*.) Sí, sí, sí, estoyyyyyy biennn.

PAPÁ: (*Entra con una tortilla*.) ¡Huele a carne asada! ¿Ya esta la carne?

DOÑA ROTA: Sé está muriendo el Señor Estasbien.

ESTASBIEN: Estoy bien, no se preocupen. No puedo sentir mis brazos pero estoy bien. ¿A ver donde estábamos? Bueno, hay que asegurarnos

162

que no haya nada de objetos o juguetes pequeños que el bebé se puede meter a la boca. Especialmente globos de hule. Globos como estos (*Tiene un globo y se lo pone junto a la boca.*) causan un tercio de todas las muertes en bebés que se ahogan. (*Trata de inflar el globo y empieza a ahogarse.*)

DOÑA ROTA: ¿Está bien?

PAPÁ: Dí algo. ¿Señor está bien?

ESTASBIEN: (*Escribe con una pluma en un papel.*) No estoy bien.

DOÑA ROTA: Viejo, haz algo. No está bien el Señor Estasbien.

PAPÁ: Deténmelo. (Papá *lo agarra y lo levanta por atrás y lo suelta. Luego* Estasbien *se saca el globo de la boca.*)

ESTASBIEN: (*Se cae al piso, luego se levanta.*) Gracias, señor. Gracias. Bueno es muy importante que uno tome clases de primeros auxilios para saber como ayudar a una persona si sé está ahogando con algo. Infórmese donde usted puede tomar clases para aprender la manera correcta de dar RCP o CPR. Es importante saber cuando un niño se está ahogando. El mejor indicador es cuando el niño no puede toser, hablar o si cambia de color.

PAPÁ: Yo puedo ser un maestro, Señor Estasbien.

ESTASBIEN: Bueno, después hablamos sobre esto. Creo que me quebré una costilla. Si uno vive en una casa de dos pisos o en un apartamento que no está en el primer piso, es muy importante no poner sillones junto a las ventanas. Cada año muchos bebés se mueren cuando se caen de la ventana. También, puede comprar un coral para que los niños no se caigan de las escaleras. No es recomendado usar "andad eras", son muy peligrosas cuando se voltean. Los bebes se pueden quebrar un brazo o lastimar la cabeza. Yo cuando era chico me caí de una andadera y me tuvieron que poner 400 puntadas en la cabeza pero estoy bien. (*Camina a la cocina.*) El lugar más peligroso de la casa es la cocina. Aquí hay muchas cosas que pueden lastimar a su hijo. Un bebé nunca debe de estar en la cocina cuando alguien está cocinando. El agua caliente es un gran peligro. (*Agarra la olla con agua caliente y se le voltea por accidente. Empieza a gritar.*) ¡Aaagghhh! ¡Aayyy!

DOÑA ROTA: (*Toma hielo del refrigerador y intenta ponérselo.*) ¿Señor, está bien?

ESTASBIEN: No, no. Hielo no, ¡por favor! No se debe de poner hielo en una quemada. Se pone agua fría y después una crema para las quemaduras. Bueno, estoy bien. Si no tienen crema, la sábila es muy buena para las quemadas. Los cuchillos son otro gran peligro para sus niños. (Doña Rota *está cortando lechuga cuando suelta el cuchillo y se lo entra a la frente de* Estasbien.)

DOÑA ROTA: ¡Ay dios mío! Ya maté al Señor Estasbien! (Estasbien *se levanta del piso.*)

ESTASBIEN: Estoy bien, estoy bien. (*Tiene el cuchillo atorado en la frente.*) ¿A ver, dónde estaba? Asegúrese que los niños no estén al alcance de ningún tipo de medicina. Muchas veces los niños piensan que son dulces y se las toman. Es importante cerrar todos los lugares que tengan Ajax u otros productos que usan para limpiar la casa. Se pueden cerrar con algo muy sencillo como esto y no cuesta mucho en las tiendas. Tenga a su alcance el número telefónico de la agencia de control de veneno, una llamada a ellos puede salvarle la vida a su hijo. Otro lugar muy peligroso es el baño. Vamos al baño. (*Toca la puerta del baño.*)

PAPÁ: Un momento. (*Sale del baño y* Estasbien *se desmaya.*) Híjole, vieja creo que Juan Estasbien no está muy bien...apúrate, trae agua.

DOÑA ROTA: (*Entra con un vaso de agua y se lo echa encima a* Estasbien.) Y tú, ¿qué estabas haciendo en este baño? Este es mi show.

PAPÁ: Es el único baño que pude encontrar.

DOÑA ROTA: ¡Aaaayyy! ¡Viejo, me tienes harta! ¿Señor Estasbien, está bien?

ESTASBIEN: Estoy bien, estoy bien. ¿A ver, dónde estaba? No sé qué pasó, no me acuerdo de nada, nomás un olor muy fuerte. Bueno, bueno. Sí, el baño es muy peligroso. En muchos casos los niños chicos se han ahogado en la taza del baño. Pueden comprar un candado como éste y ponérselo para proteger al niño. Cuando estén bañando al niño, toque el agua primero usted, que no esté muy caliente o fría. No dejen que los niños se laven las manos solos hasta que ya estén más grandes y entiendan bien cual es el agua caliente y fría. Y también no dejen a los niños solos en la tina hasta que ya tengan más de cinco años. Los niños se pueden ahogar muy rápido. Cada año miles de niños se ahogan en una alberca. Un pequeño descuido y su hijo puede ahogarse. (*Están cerca de una alberca chica de niños y se cae* Estasbien *en la alberca.*)

DOÑA ROTA: (*Grita.*) Y ahora, ¿quién podrá ayudarnos? (*En ese momento empieza la música de* Baywatch *y el* Papá *sale en cámara lenta con un sorel y con un salvavidas.*)

ESTASBIEN: No sé nadar. ¡Mamá, me voy ahogar, mamá! ¡Ayúdame Santo, ayúdame!

Teatro Izcalli DOÑA ROTA: ¿No que no, viejo? Ves, ¡él si cree en el Santo! (*Tira el juguete del Santo en la alberca y está amarrado con un hilo.* Estasbien *se agarae del Santo y lo sacan para afuera.*)

PAPÁ: (*Levanta al Santo del piso.*) Gracias Santo, gracias. Le salvaste la vida.

DOÑA ROTA: Te dije, viejo, que el Santo si es salvavidas. ¿Está bien, Señor Estasbien?

ESTASBIEN: Estoy bien, estoy bien, estoy bien. (*Volviéndose loco.*) Sí mamá, me gusta el chocolate. No, no, Chancla, perra mala no hagas eso. Si mamá, me gustan los tamales. ¡No, Chancla! ¿Qué estés haciendo con mi pierna? Estoy bien, estoy bien. Bueno, la última cosa que les digo. Por favor, si tienen una pistola en la casa hay que asegurarse que tenga candado la pistola y nunca debe de estar cargada en la casa. La pistola y las balas deben de estar separadas.

PAPÁ: Yo tengo una pistola. ¿Quiere que la traiga para que de una muestra?

ESTASBIEN: No, no gracias señor. Estoy bien. (*Se va corriendo.*)

DOÑA ROTA: Adiós. Muchas gracias. ¡Que buen muchacho! ¿Verdad, viejo?

PAPÁ: Sí. ¿Cómo dijiste que se llamaba?

DOÑA ROTA: Ay no sé. Con todo lo que pasó, se me olvidó su nombre.

(*Fin.*)

0 a 5 Grant commissioned by Chicano Federation, 2003.
Left: Ramon "Chunky" Sanchez, Olympia Rodriguez, Iyari Arteaga, Alicia Chavez, Jose Alvarez, Claudia Cuevas, and Macedonio Arteaga Jr.
Photo by Juan Carlos Sanchez.

commissioned works

In 2007, we were commissioned to write and perform a play on Cinco de Mayo by the South Bay Cinco de Mayo Con Orgullo Coalition. The goal of the Cinco de Mayo Con Orgullo Coalition is to educate others about the exploitation and alcohol marketing practices regarding this holiday in the Latino community. We wrote a play called Juan More Beer and have performed it in May for the past two years. The play is not featured in this book since it's still a work in progress.

Juan More Beer, 2008.
Back left: Michael Slomanson, Jose Alvarez, Hector Villegas, Claudia Cuevas. Front left: Macedonio Arteaga Jr., Alicia Chavez, and Iyari Arteaga.
Photo by Karla Solorio. Flyer design by Abraham Jimenez.

Teatro Izcalli